Praise for
Hear the Savior

I find it tough to connect with many devotionals because they often seem like someone's formulaic opinion of a verse (sometimes out of context). But, as a former pastor, I'm impressed by Kristin Saatzer's theological rigor. Proper theology can be dry and boring, but her applications and personal stories keep the Bible at the forefront while helping the reader apply Jesus's words to their lives. I highly recommend this devotional on the most important living words from the most important living Person.

—Chris Fogle, author of *Biblical Knowledge, Understanding & Wisdom* and staff writer for Christ and Pop Culture

You're not just holding a devotional. You're holding a book of devotion. Besides being a woman of excellence, Kristin is devoted to God and His message. I have witnessed first hand her dedication to getting the words on these pages. Your Lent, Easter, and view of our mighty God will never be the same.

Even if you've grown up celebrating the true meaning of Easter, Kristin brings a fresh perspective with her personal stories of grace and hope. Besides the countless hours of research and study, I have personally seen her heart for God's Word pouring out on these pages as she wrote. The perfect book to elevate your Easter season.

—Carrie Talbott VomSteeg, blogger and author of *Pete and His Gigantic Feet*

i

Hear the Savior is such a powerful and challenging devotional. I kept wanting to skip ahead to the next day to see what I was going to be learning about. The way the book teaches about Jesus's journey and interactions with people is so relevant and timely in how we live life today. The daily reflections with each devotion will take you from learning a deeper insight about Jesus to how to practically use this in your daily faith journey. This is a great book for those who are new to faith or seeking to learn about Jesus and it is written in a way that it will challenge those mature in their faith to want to grow closer to Him each day.

I can't wait to share this with the coaches in our athletic department and give each of my players a book!

—James Gleghorn, Associate Athletic Director and
Men's and Women's Tennis Coach,
Indiana Wesleyan University

In *Hear the Savior* Kristin Saatzer skillfully weaves a scholarly biblical background, facts, and insights during the 40 days of Lent, while also walking alongside Jesus in a very personal way. One reads this inspired to be transformed as a Jesus-follower but also given tools to be equipped to do so, daily. Kristin's transparency with chronic illness, personal struggles, and reflections furthers the reader to make focused applications in the profound quotes, daily Reflection section, and closing Prayer. I highly recommend this book!

—Sue Smedley, Spiritual Formation Director,
Rivendell Institute at Yale

HEAR
the
SAVIOR

Readings for Lent and Easter
Based on the Words of Jesus

HEAR
the
SAVIOR

Readings for Lent and Easter
Based on the Words of Jesus

Kristin Saatzer

REDEMPTION
PRESS

I dedicate this book to you, Jeni, my sister and best friend. Our hearts are tightly tied. You are a beautiful example of one who heeds the Savior's words, and I thank you for your unending encouragement and support. I love you.

Contents

Judea and Perea

Holy Week

The Risen Savior

Preface

Blessed Jesus, at Thy Word
(verse 1)

Blessed Jesus, at your word
we are gathered all to hear you.
Let our hearts and souls be stirred
now to seek and love and fear you.
By your gospel pure and holy,
teach us, Lord, to love you solely.[1]

Dear friend,

I began the year 2020 with plans to start and finish my second book. How could I (or any of us) have known that a global pandemic was on the horizon? When life shut down, I suddenly had time on my hands to work on my project, but my house grew busy as my kids came home and we all hunkered down together. I did begin and finally finished this book during the years of COVID-19 craziness, distractions, interruptions, a lengthy illness, and family togetherness. But it took much longer than I anticipated.

I spent countless hours reading the Gospels and researching what scholars had to say about what Jesus had to say. This amateur theologian took in a ton of theology, and the pages you hold in your hands are my humble attempt to listen in on and become intimate with the words of our Savior. I am deeply grateful you have decided to join me.

---

[1] Tobias Clausnitzer, "Blessed Jesus, at Thy Word," 1707.

As we begin our trek together, there are a few things I'd like to cover. First, Jesus had a lot to say! Each word is infused in love. There is too much to fit in one book, and I wrestled with what to include and leave out. So I encourage you to do your own study and read the Gospels and let Him speak to you in the gaps of what we could not study together.

Second, this book is written with an Easter focus, in chronological order, with the Lenten season pointing us to Christ's death and resurrection. Therefore, I believe it would be helpful for us to look at the meaning of Lent.

Lent (noun):

The 40 weekdays from Ash Wednesday to Easter observed by the Roman Catholic, Eastern, and some Protestant churches as a period of penitence and fasting[2]

Lent is not in the Bible, but it is one of the oldest church traditions on the Christian calendar, possibly dating back to 325 and the First Council of Nicaea. It has changed over the years, but its purpose has endured as a time of self-examination with prayer, confession, repentance, and Scripture reading. And as a time for self-denial, usually with fasting, in preparation for Easter. Various theologians claim Lent was modeled after the forty days the Messiah spent in the wilderness fasting and praying.

The purpose of these disciplines is not to punish ourselves for our sins. Jesus took all the punishment for us. Rather, the

---

[2] "Lent," *Merriam-Webster.com*, 2022, https://www.merriam-webster.com/dictionary/lent.

disciplines are meant to empty us, so there the Lord will fill us. We are making ourselves available to Christ in hopes of growing our faith.[3]

Not all Christian traditions observe Lent. I did not observe Lent in my childhood church or in the churches of my adult life. I have taken up this practice in recent years, and it may be new to you as well. There are no rules. Perhaps you'll choose to fast from certain foods or certain meals. How about giving up social media or TV for forty days? Think about what spiritual practice you might replace this vacancy with or what you'll make room for instead. You can add a discipline like reading the Bible or a spiritual book like this one each day of Lent or memorize Scripture. People often fast as a time of remembrance and dependence on their Savior. It is a period of reflection, to show love toward Him, and to grow deeper in faith.

For our purposes, to line up our reading to end on Easter, count backward forty days from Easter Sunday and start day one of this book on that day. Even though many traditions begin on Ash Wednesday (taking Sundays off), we will go forty days straight to Easter Sunday (with a couple of post-Easter readings at the end of the book).

If you are late to start, jump in wherever it works for you during the Lenten season. Actually, you can read this book any time of the year, as Christ's words are there for us no matter the season.

I pray that you will carve out time each day to be alone with Christ and receive what He has for you. Fill yourself up in His love. Ask yourself, "How do the words of Jesus relate to me today?"

---

[3] Father Thomas McKenzie, *The Anglican Way* (Nashville, TN: Rabbit Room, 2014).

Reflect deeply and use a notebook, journal, or the space provided in the book to answer the questions after each devotional.

My friend, may you grow in love, knowledge, and intimacy with your Savior.

Blessings,
Kristin

Days 1-6
Early Ministry

Turn Your Eyes upon Jesus
(Verses 1, 3, and Refrain)

O soul, are you weary and troubled?
No light in the darkness you see?
There's light for a look at the Savior,
And life more abundant and free!

His Word shall not fail you—He promised;
Believe Him, and all will be well:
Then go to a world that is dying,
His perfect salvation to tell!

Turn your eyes upon Jesus,
Look full in His wonderful face,
And the things of earth will grow strangely dim,
In the light of His glory and grace.[4]

---

[4]   Helen Howarth Lemmel, "Turn Your Eyes upon Jesus," 1922.

#1

Famous First Words

"Why did you need to search?" he asked.
"Didn't you know that I must be in my Father's house?"
But they didn't understand what he meant.
Luke 2:49–50 (NLT)

He's not here!

One day at the park, as I stood up after helping my toddler tie his shoe, my breath caught in my throat as I realized his five-year-old brother had slipped away. My eyes flashed around to the sand and play structure—no sign of Sammy. As my heart pounded in my ears, I shouted his name, and others joined the search. After about five panicked-parent minutes, a man yelled out. Then Sammy, quite a distance off, sheepishly crawled out of a hole. I ran to my boy and squeezed him tight—my heart slow to recover—as I admonished him for wandering away.

In the pages of the Bible, we discover a story of parents whose son also slipped off. Mary and Joseph could not find twelve-year-old Jesus, and their panicked-parent minutes turned into days. Can you even imagine?

The family traveled from Jerusalem in a large caravan to their hometown of Nazareth after the annual Passover celebration. Mom and Dad presumed Jesus was in the company of relatives or friends. Once they realized their boy was not with the group, the parents swiftly headed back to Jerusalem to look for Jesus.

After a three-day search, they found Him sitting in the temple with the teachers, asking questions. Those gathered around this lost boy were amazed by His knowledge, as were His parents. After His mother admonished Him and asked Him why He had treated them inconsiderately, Jesus questioned her, curious as to why they needed to search for Him. He wondered why she did not know He was in His Father's house.

These words of Jesus to Mary are the first recorded words spoken by Jesus Christ. Famous first words.

It's quite a scene: relieved and confused parents, genius kid, astonished crowd, profound questions ... a lot going on. As a mom, my instinct is that Mary should've punished her son big time. No phone, no friends, no privileges. But this was not your typical scene, and this was not your typical tween. Here was the young Savior, His heart already solid in adoration for His Father in heaven.

As Luke 2:52 tells us, the family then returned home, where Jesus obeyed His parents, grew in wisdom and stature and in favor with people and God. Yet the first brick on the road to the cross was paved that day in the temple with the questions of Christ. The allegiance of the only begotten Son shifted from earth to heaven.

> The personal intimacy of the phrase "my Father" referring to God is unprecedented in Jewish literature, where it might be expressed as "in heaven" or "our Father." It is this amazing claim of intimate filial relationship to the Father that gets him accused of blasphemy later in life. (John 10:29–39)[5]

---

5   Dr. Ralph F. Wilson, "The Boy Jesus in the Temple (Luke 2:39–52)," www. Jesuswalk.com/luke/apx1h-boy-jesus.htm.

Reflection

1. What are your intentions and expectations as you begin to read this book and study the Savior's words? Write them as a prayer.

2. Commit to spending a few quiet moments with your Savior each day of the Easter season in reading, reflection, and prayer.

Prayer

Dear Savior,

Here we go! I commit this journey to You. Thank You for these first recorded words of Yours, where I get to see a snapshot of You as a boy, a someday-Savior who intimately adored His Father. A Son who prepared for His purpose on this earth: to love and to die for His beloved.

Amen

#2

The Wilderness

He answered, "It is written,
'Man shall not live by bread alone,
but by every word that comes from the mouth of God.'" ...
"Again it is written,
'You shall not put the Lord your God to the test.'" ...
"Be gone, Satan! For it is written,
'You shall worship the Lord your God
and him only shall you serve.'"
Matthew 4:4, 7, 10 (ESV)

I grabbed my phone from the nightstand once again; 3:34 AM flashed menacingly at me. Yet another night to declare insomnia the winner and me the loser. How many nights, how many *weeks* had it been since I had slept more than a couple of hours? How long had it been since I'd felt like myself? Black shadows of months in a wilderness had taken hold of me—mentally, physically, and worst of all, spiritually. It seemed God was nowhere to be found.

You may be staggering through your own spiritual wilderness as you read these words, wandering the backwoods of your brain, wondering where Jesus is. If not now, maybe in your past somewhere. A desert experience that haunts you sometimes. Perhaps a trial waits for you beyond the next turn.

Our Savior endured a time in the wilderness after His baptism by John and was prompted by the Spirit of God to go to the hills of the Judean desert. After forty days of fasting and ministry preparation, Satan confronted Christ with a series of temptations.

Each time the enemy challenged Him, Christ responded with Scripture, and it was no match for Satan. God's Word is a weapon in times of weakness.

In the weakest, bleakest hours in my walk through the wilderness, when I could not feel God, I knew to pull out His Word. Sitting with my Bible on my lap, I paged through familiar truths as I prayed that God would show Himself anew in my life. That His mercy would shine on me and strengthen me in my desolate place of pain.

The good news is, Jesus endured His temptation. As we read in Matthew's gospel (*gospel* means "good news"), Satan fled after his attempts to tempt Jesus failed. God's mercy abounded.

Our Creator has not left us alone and unarmed in the hands of the enemy. God was present in every moment of Christ's days in the Judean desert as He is present in our lives today. Even in seasons where we do not "feel" Him, we can remind ourselves that God Almighty became "God with us" (Matthew 1:23) through His Son.

My wilderness season stretched long, and it simply became a practice of endurance. Yet eventually I began to feel a bit like myself again and the gift of sleep won over insomnia more and more.

As I continued in His Word and uttered my small prayers, my heart began to change. My union with Him shifted to a connected, vibrant walk once more.

It is good news that His mercy abounds, and His comfort may be found in our happiest and hardest wilderness days.

He who lives in us is greater! Sometimes we forget that we do
not fight against flesh and blood, but against principalities
and evil powers (Ephesians 6:12). We desperately need to
remember whose we are and how to fight.[6]

Reflection

1. Read the entirety of the temptation of Jesus in Matthew
    4:1–11.

2. How might this passage empower you in your own
    personal wilderness?

Prayer

Dear Savior,

Your mercy abounds in my wilderness seasons. Where would
I be without You? Thank You for resisting Satan, for the victory in
the desolate place, and for Your comfort and care in my happy and
hard days.

Amen

---

6   Sheila Walsh, *The Storm Inside: Trade the Chaos of How You Feel for the Truth of Who You Are* (Nashville, TN: HarperCollins Christian Publishing, 2014).

#3

The Learners

"What do you seek?" ...
"Come and see." ...
"Follow Me."
John 1:38, 39, 43 (NKJV)

Disciple (noun):
A convinced adherent of a school or individual[7]

Mary's son was thirty years old when He left His hometown of Nazareth to revolutionize the world. After John baptized Jesus in the Jordan River, the ministry wheels were set in motion. Two of John's disciples left the Jordan to join the one whom John the Baptist called "the Lamb of God" (John 1:29, 36).

Quickly, this charismatic rabbi attracted attention and admirers. As He engaged with the men who would later become His closest companions, He asked them questions. He encouraged them to examine His message and called them to an intimate expedition with Him as disciples. As learners.

Each day of our Easter walk together, dive into Christ's message and place yourself in the pages. You've left hearth and

---

[7] "Disciple," *Merriam-Webster.com*, 2022, https://www.merriam-webster.com/dictionary/disciple.

home as a devotee of a new-on-the-job preacher on the dusty roads of Israel. Sit next to Him on the grass, track close to His footprints, lean in with ears wide open to learn as you never have before.

Today, dear learner, consider and personalize the following words of our Savior:

1. *What do you seek?* When the disciples of John departed the river to accompany Christ, He turned around and asked them this poignant question.

   Study your heart:
   What am I seeking to learn from the Savior this spring?

2. *Come and see!* Look with your own eyes. Jesus gave His disciples an opportunity to go with Him immediately, to check out where He lived, and to converse and study with Him for the day.

   Observe in yourself:
   How can I open my eyes to the Savior in new ways?

3. *Follow Me.* The next day, as Jesus prepared to leave for Galilee, He spoke this charge of action to a man named Phillip: *Be My disciple.* This weighty summons was a stretched-out hand for Phillip to grasp. Here, he recognized the rabbi as more than a teacher but as the Savior of the World.

   Ponder this:
   Have I chosen to follow Christ as my teacher and my Savior?

In the first century, a teacher often extended an invitation to a prospective disciple who showed promise, not necessarily because the student received all A's on his essays or kept his school desk in perfect order. Our Lord saw potential in a motley group of imperfect, unqualified, ordinary men and bade them to come and track His steps, to sit by His side as they learned from Him and matured into His likeness.

He qualified them after He called them.

In the twenty-first century, Jesus summons us to grasp His hand and pursue our destiny. We C students with messy desks. The imperfect, ordinary, and unqualified. Learners maturing into His likeness.

We are qualified because of His call.

> Jesus called the twelve not for who they were
> but for who they were to become.[8]

Reflection

1. Thoughtfully write out your answers to the three preceding questions.

2. Commit to God in prayer to learn as you never have before in these coming weeks.

---

[8] A. B. Bruce, *The Training of the Twelve: How Jesus Christ Found and Taught the 12 Apostles; A Book of New Testament Biography* (Scotts Valley, CA: CreateSpace, 2018).

Prayer

Dear Savior,

I choose to seek, to come and see, and to follow You. Thank You for Your outstretched hand and for the open spot on the grass by Your side. I am Your disciple, and in You I am qualified. Therefore, I commit to learn from You as never before.

Amen

#4
Mother and Son

Jesus said to her, "Woman, what does this have to do
with me? My hour has not yet come."
John 2:4 (ESV)

Laughter erupted as music soaked the air. Friends and family
sipped wine and dined on fresh fish while the bride and groom
joyfully gazed on. Among the guests were Christ, His new
disciples, and His family.

I adore this image of Jesus laughing and joking and living it
up. I think our Savior loved fun. The story gets even better (to
me as the mother of boys) because the writer tells us Christ was
hanging out with His mom at this wedding in Cana. I am all in for
mother-son stories, though this one confuses me.

The party was far from over, but the wine was gone. Not good.
When Mary informed her son that the vino was no more, His reply
appears disrespectful, as if He were irritated. He does not call her
mother or *ma'am*, or even Mary, but *Woman*.

Commentators (mostly) agree that the word used here, *gynai*
in the Greek language, is a respectful form of address. Yet there
are no other accounts in Scripture of someone using this name for
one's own mother. *Except one.* Mary's beloved child uttered this
term of endearment on a second occasion, this time from the cross:
"Woman, here is your son" (John 19:26).

My curiosity piques in the next part of the sentence: Christ's question. Did the Messiah want His mom to leave Him alone in His laughter, food, and conversation? Did He not want to be bothered with something that should have been the host's responsibility?

I am intrigued further by the next statement. He said His hour had not yet come. To what hour was He referring? The time for miracles? Why was Christ reluctant to act?

Even though His ministry had barely begun, I believe this mom knew who Her child was destined to become. She had a foretaste of His fate from the angel and the wise men. Then from Simeon and Anna in the temple (see Luke chapters 1 and 2).

So this was to be more than a party trick performance. Somehow, some way, Mary knew it was time for her child to begin the fulfillment of His destiny. After their exchange, a confident Mary told the servants, "Do whatever he tells you" (John 2:5).

Then, even in Christ's apparent reluctance to act, He acted. Water became premium wine. At the end of this story, John tells us this was the first of Christ's miraculous signs. In the Bible, a sign is a miracle with deeper meaning, intended to convey truths that would not otherwise be known.

This sign, shown through water and wine, reveals the sovereignty and mystery of the living God. Here Mary models a sensitivity to the work of God and a belief in His power.

I still do not understand the mystery of why this story played out as it did. However, I like to think this son did what He did when He did it because His mama asked Him to.

Miracles are a retelling in small letters of the very same story which is written across the whole world in letters too large for some of us to see.[9]

---

[9]   C. S. Lewis, *Miracles* (San Francisco, CA: HarperOne, 2009).

Reflection

1. In what ways does this story speak to you about God's mystery and power?

2. Read John 19:25–27 and compare this passage to the story of Jesus's first miracle. Record your thoughts.

Prayer

Dear Savior,

Thank You for revealing Your first miracle in a fun family setting and for displaying a side of You that shows the multiple dimensions of Your humanity, divinity, mystery, and sovereignty.

Amen

#5

For God So Loved the World

For God so loved the world,
that He gave His only Son, so that everyone
who believes in Him will not perish, but have eternal life.
John 3:16 (NASB)

He came by night.

In the early days of Jesus's ministry, a Pharisee approached Him under the cloak of darkness. Perhaps this religious leader was afraid his colleagues wouldn't approve of his meeting this young man from Nazareth who did *not* abide by the rules. The Pharisees were a legalistic Jewish sect; they followed a strict observance of traditional law and were known for their self-righteousness.

Yet Nicodemus was drawn to Christ, curious and stirred, so he took the risk. He complimented Jesus in his greeting: "Rabbi, we know that You have come from God as a teacher; for no one can do these signs that You do unless God is with him" (John 3:2 NASB). But Jesus was not flattered.

And then came the boom. The gospel of grace spelled out by its author and perfecter. As the Savior spoke, Nicodemus grew agitated and asked how these things could be. Jesus pointed out that Nicodemus was a teacher of Israel, and even still, he could not understand. Both a paradox and a tragedy. Jesus said to him:

> Truly, truly, I say to you, we speak of what we know and testify of what we have seen, and you people do not accept our testimony. If I told you earthly things and you do not believe, how will you believe if I tell you heavenly things? No one has ascended into heaven, except He who descended from heaven: the Son of Man. And just as Moses lifted up the serpent in the wilderness, so must the Son of Man be lifted up, so that everyone who believes will have eternal life in him. (John 3:11–15 NASB)

Here Jesus identified Himself as Messiah, with the possibility of eternal life through Himself and *not* through works.

In his religious studies and obsession with the law, Nicodemus had missed the truth of grace.

Until that night.

Then comes possibly the most well-known passage of Scripture, our key verse today, John 3:16. "For God so loved the world ..." The truths contained in these words of Christ are life-altering. Simple, yes. Easy? Maybe not. Especially for one like Nicodemus, who'd spent his life following rules and attempting to live as a religious man.

Eventually, Nicodemus gave his allegiance to the Messiah. The last we see of him is in John 19, verses 39 and 40, aiding in the burial of Christ.

The secret to eternal life is not laws, rules, or self-righteous piety. It cannot be earned, as it comes only by belief in the Son of God. Not just for the undercover curious Pharisee but for us too.

The ones who come with questions by day and in fear by night. The gospel of grace is a gift, ours for the taking. The gospel of grace is the gospel of ultimate love.

Because God *so* loved the world ...

> Nicodemus knew how to march, but he longed to sing. He knew there was something more, but he didn't know where to find it. So he went to Jesus.[10]

Reflection

1. Have you embraced and accepted this gospel of grace?

2. Read John 6:40, John 11:25, and Romans 5:8. Journal the truths you find and thank your Savior for them.

Prayer

Dear Savior,

As You, the only begotten Son of God, extend Your hand in grace to me, I accept it. A gift too inexplicable to understand. Yet, like Nicodemus, I choose the way of grace. My allegiance is to You. Thank You for saving me.

Amen

---

[10] Max Lucado, *He Still Moves Stones* (Nashville, TN: Thomas Nelson, 2013).

#6

Unexpected

Whoever drinks the water I give them will never thirst.
Indeed, the water I give them will become in them a
spring of water welling up to eternal life.
John 4:14

Tongues were wagging, and He'd barely begun. A group of Jewish leaders resented His rise in popularity, but it was too soon for Christ to challenge them in the open. To avoid them, He chose a short but atypical route out of Judea and trod north through Samaria.

Samaria, Jesus? The Jews usually took the long way around because bad blood between the Jews and the Samaritans boiled hot. Seven hundred years of searing prejudice percolated in the hearts of the Jews toward their northern neighbors, because the Samaritans were only part Jew, considered a mixed race. Unclean. But the unpredictable Savior did not play the brutish game of bigotry.

So, under the sizzling midday sun, a weary Jesus stopped for rest and refreshment at a place called Jacob's Well. At the same time, a lone Samaritan woman carrying an empty water jug headed His way. An immoral woman of societal disgrace who chose the hottest hour of the day to fill her jug because it was likely she would meet no one.

Yet a man was there. A lone *Jewish* man. And He spoke directly to her. I imagine her heart flipped and her throat tightened as He looked into her eyes and voiced the following unexpected statements found in John chapter 4:

"Give me a drink" (verse 7): A Jew asked for water from her, an unknown woman (women in this time were considered to be lower class than men) of another race.

"He would have given you living water" (verse 10): This stranger used water as a metaphor and promised her eternal life.

"Go, call your husband and come back" (verse 16): An astonishing man knew her history, that she'd had five husbands and was living with a man she was not married to.

"I, the one speaking to you—I am he" (verse 26): A Nazarene who declared Himself to be the Messiah.

My soul stirs with wonder as I consider the value our scandalous Savior placed on one solitary soul. That He would break the bonds of the expected, see her need, and reveal Himself in this intimate way as the Water of Life. Her Water of Life.

This story compels me to open my eyes wide to one solitary soul in my life, someone needing an unexpected expression of care. A beloved child of God who could use a cool drink of water after traveling alone in a desolate place.

I want to pass along the cup of Christ.

The woman from the well did this. Her joy spilled over, and she told others about her encounter. Then an entire village was transformed as their cups overflowed with water from the Well of Eternal Life.

> They said to the woman, "We no longer believe just because of
> what you said; now we have heard for ourselves, and we know
> that this man really is the Savior of the world."
> John 4:42

Reflection

1. There is much to unpack in this section of Scripture, and I encourage you to jump into John 4:1–41 on your own.

2. Think about one person in your life to surprise with an act of love this week.

Prayer

Dear Savior,

You are the God of surprises! I am compelled by Your love as I open my eyes to see who needs some unexpected care in this season of Easter.

Amen

Days 7-26
Galilee

Jesus Calls Us
(Verses 1, 2, and 3)

Jesus calls us o'er the tumult
of our life's wild, restless sea;
day by day his voice invites me,
saying, "Christian, follow me!"

As the first disciples heard it
by the Galilean lake,
turned from home and toil and kindred,
leaving all for his dear sake.

Jesus calls us from the worship
of the vain world's golden store,
from each idol that would keep us,
saying, "Christian, love me more."[11]

---

[11]   Cecil Frances Alexander, "Jesus Calls Us," 1852.

#7

Signs and Wonders and Words

"Unless you people see signs and wonders,"
Jesus told him, "you will never believe."
John 4:48

After the revival in Samaria, the Messiah journeyed to Cana in Galilee. Here He performed His first of twenty-seven recorded healing miracles.

A father walked twenty desperate miles to find Jesus. When he found Christ, he begged Him to heal his beloved son, who was near death. This man was a high government official who most likely worked for King Herod Antipas—not your ordinary Hebrew fisherman. Yet all needy believers are equalized at the feet of the Healer.

The royal official said, "Sir, come down before my child dies" (John 4:49).

Christ did not immediately respond to the father's request for help. Instead He admonished this father and the crowd by declaring that they would not believe in Him unless He performed signs and wonders. I find the Savior's terse response to this man worth pondering. Did He feel frustrated because of the disparity between the Jews and the Samaritans? It seems the Jews were only interested in miraculous acts to prove His deity, but the Samaritans believed through His words.

The Messiah tested the official's faith by not performing an outward sign of healing. Instead, He compelled the man to believe in His word alone.

"'Go,' Jesus replied, 'your son will live.' The man took Jesus at his word and departed." (John 4:50)

Christ desires much more for His beloved than a faith that seeks only the miraculous.

When God made the universe, He spoke. And in the opening of John's gospel, we are introduced to God's Son this way: "In the beginning was the Word, and the Word was with God, and the Word was God" (John 1:1). Further along it says, "The Word became flesh and made his dwelling among us" (John 1:14).

The Son of God, called the Word, is the physical manifestation of God the Father. And the Word spoke astonishing, life-breathing kingdom proclamations into the world.

So words are a huge deal to God. Yet are they a huge deal to us? Or are we like the early followers of Jesus, looking for massive signs and spectacles before we trust Him? As we view the handiwork of God, we must remember that the Bible itself is a sign and a wonder. It is not mere words; it is God-breathed, and God still speaks to us. This is a huge deal, so I will say it again— God speaks to us!

And that, my friend, is a miracle.

As we move along together, may we daily marvel at the wonder of His Word, remembering that Christ not only spoke to His followers then, on the dusty streets of Cana, but He speaks to His followers now, on our own spot on the globe.

On his way back, his servants intercepted him and announced,
"Your son lives!" He asked them what time he began to get
better. They said, "The fever broke yesterday afternoon at one
o'clock." The father knew that that was the very moment Jesus
had said, "Your son lives." That settled it. Not only he but his
entire household believed.

John 4:52–53 (MSG)

Reflection

1. In what areas do you expect a wonder instead of taking
   the Savior at His word?

2. For further study, read 2 Samuel 23:2, Romans 15:4, and
   2 Timothy 3:16.

Prayer

Dear Savior,

Thank You for the marvelous wonder of Your words and that
You speak to me! In turn, I will proclaim Your life-giving words to
others.

Amen

#8

Purpose

Now when it was day, He departed and went into a
deserted place. And the crowd sought Him and came to
Him, and tried to keep Him from leaving them; but He
said to them, "I must preach the kingdom of God to the
other cities also, because for this purpose I have been
sent." And He was preaching in the synagogues of Galilee.
Luke 4:42–44 (NKJV)

Purpose (noun):
1. Something set up as an object or end to be attained
2. Resolution; determination[12]

Jesus was gaining popularity in Galilee, and followers increasingly
flocked as the days passed, but it was time to leave them and
journey to Judea. Early one morning, as He sought solitude to
refuel and talk with God, the crowds found Him. They attempted
to convince Him to remain in Galilee, to not move on to other
places. But because Jesus knew His purpose, He followed the
timeline God put before Him, His to-do list always in His
pocket.

---

[12] "Purpose," *Merriam-Webster.com*, 2022, https://www.merriam-webster.com/
dictionary/purpose.

Thus, He left the Galilean crowds and trod the dusty seventy-mile trek to Judea.

The Messiah spent three and a half years on assignment. He rested and ate. He spent time with friends and stole away to be alone with His Father. I don't think Jesus would have gotten involved in long group texts or checked social media each time He stopped for water. A single-minded Savior, He was committed to making the most of His time.

So what exactly was the aim and mission of the Son of God? Why did the Father send Him to us? The Word of God tells us He came:

- To heal the sick (Luke 5:12–15)
- To seek and save the lost (Luke 19:10)
- To die for our sins and to rise again (Luke 24:46)
- To call His followers to an abundant life (John 10:10)

For these purposes He was born. For these assignments He was called.

As a child of God, you too are called to a specific mission. He created you fearfully and wonderfully to care for the sick. To give to the poor. To seek the lonely and lost with the message of eternal life and the hope of Jesus. To shine the light of God's grace in your world, in your way. To live in community.

This is the abundant life.

Let's make the most of the Easter season by following in the Savior's steps, walking out our purpose and our calling in the world, in our way.

Only One Life

Give me, Father, a purpose deep,
In joy or sorrow Thy word to keep;
Faithful and true whate'er the strife,
Pleasing Thee in my daily life.

Only one life, 'twill soon be past.
Only what's done for Christ will last.[13]

Reflection

1. Read Philippians 3:10–11 in the Amplified version and pledge these words as your truth.

2. Write one practical way to live out your calling this Easter season and beyond.

Prayer

Dear Savior,

You were born for us: to save, to heal, to die, and to rise. I am astounded by and deeply grateful for You. Thank You that I too was born for a reason. I vow to make my one life count, to love others for Your glory.

Amen

---

[13]   C. T. Studd, "Only One Life."

#9

Healer of Body and Soul

When Jesus saw their faith, he said to the paralyzed man,
"Son, your sins are forgiven."
Mark 2:5

I want you to know that the Son of Man
has authority on earth to forgive sins.
Mark 2:10

Dirt and rubble fell through the roof onto the large group of people. (Some scholars say this was Peter's home.) They had gathered to listen to the rabbi teach, and it was standing room only. Even the courtyard outside the doorway overflowed with onlookers. I imagine Jesus holding back laughter as He stopped His preaching to watch the scene unfold. From the now-open roof, a man was lowered down on a stretcher and placed at the feet of the Teacher. A paralyzed young man had a need that drove his friends to act. Even though the crowds said otherwise, these four friends were determined to get their paralytic friend to Christ.

Mark's gospel tells us that Jesus recognized the faith of this group when He told the paralytic his sins were forgiven. However, it was not the faith of the four stretcher carriers that saved this man. Their faith got their friend where he needed to be to encounter the living Savior personally. We all must come to Christ as individuals needing a Savior. Godly parents, Christian grandparents, or spiritual friends can't save us.

Also standing in this crowded room, probably with arms crossed, were the teachers of the law. The Savior knew their thoughts: they believed Him to be blasphemous because no one could forgive sins but God. So by calling Himself the Son of Man, Christ used this setting to divulge something about Himself in public for the first time: His deity.

After Jesus asked the religious leaders a question about forgiving sins and healing bodies (see Mark 2:9), He referred to Himself as the Son of Man. In this declaration, this charismatic rabbi claimed equality with God, that He had the authority to heal bodies *and* forgive sins. The implications of this statement were enormous. I'm sure the room grew silent once the gasping stopped.

Then, to wrap up this lesson with a perfect visual illustration, the Son of Man spoke to the paralytic. "I tell you, get up, take your mat and go home" (Mark 2:11). The man did just that, in full view of the crowd. Healed in body and soul.

When we peel back the layers of this entertaining Sunday school story, we see how vital Christian friends can be. Also, as He did with the religious leaders, He sees into our hearts and minds. Furthermore, we find the heart of Jesus here. That day, revealing Himself as the One True God, He gave priority to the paralytic's soul before addressing the condition of his body. I believe this is His priority in our day too—the state of our souls.

May we take time this Lenten season to sit with Jesus, to invite Him in as we assess the state of our souls. To clear the dirt and rubble and make way for His healing work.

We find in this healing the test and proof of Jesus's power not only as a physician of the body, but also as a healer of the soul.[14]

Reflection

1. The Son of God referred to Himself as the Son of Man more than one hundred times in the Gospels. Read Matthew 16:27, Mark 14:62, and Luke 21:27 and record your observations.

2. How is the state of your soul? Record your words as a prayer.

Prayer

Dear Savior,

You are the Son of Man, healer of body and soul. Thank You for this story and the lessons You have for me in Your Word. I also thank You for my godly friends and family. Today I acknowledge You as the One True God, the Savior of my soul, the forgiver of my sins.

Amen

---

[14] Dr. Henrietta C. Mears, *What the Bible Is All About NIV: Bible Handbook* (Ventura, CA: Regal Books, 1998), 398.

#10

Repent and Believe

"The time has come," he said.
"The kingdom of God has come near.
Repent and believe the good news!"
Mark 1:15

A gust of warm air blew off the sea as the preacher from Nazareth stood on the shore. His proclamations thundered through the throngs of those curious about Him and the followers already devoted to Him. The people of Galilee lived in a world of angst, crushed under the weight of Rome. Desperate for something new, their hopes were tied to the promised Messiah to come and save them. Luke 2:25 says they were "waiting for the consolation of Israel."

The kingdom of God was as near as possible, standing before the crowd. *He* was the one whose time had come. *He* was the "Good News" that He proclaimed. God's plan was in motion in the form of His Son, come to break the power of sin.

"Repent!"

Meanoiete is the original Greek word for *repent* used in Mark 1:15. It means "to change your mind, to think in a new way."[15] Jesus

---

[15] James Strong, *The New Strong's Exhaustive Concordance of the Bible* (Nashville, TN: Thomas Nelson, 1995).

exhorted the Galileans to change their minds; indeed, a change was crucial. Many in the crowd believed they could obtain salvation by toiling in obedience to their Jewish laws. If they worked tirelessly to follow Abraham's and Moses's commands, their external deeds would be enough to please God. Yet here, the Son of God introduced a new standard of righteousness. One based on an internal, mindful release of the old ways. One that required a Savior.

"Believe!"

Pisteuó is the Greek word used in today's Scripture for *believe*. It means "believe in, have faith in, trust in."[16] After repentance comes the next step: belief. Nothing else. No regulations, no perfect submission to the commandments, no sacrifice of offerings. Just belief. Unworthy humans receive a gift of righteousness when we believe in the one who holds the key to heaven.

As the Savior of Grace stood in the scorching sun, He summarized the method of salvation in two steps: *meanoiete* and *pisteuó*. Many in the crowd accepted His Good News summons that day and began their journey of living for Him.

The great news is that His plan is still in motion. Jesus holds out His hand in invitation to us wherever we are today. Whether you desire a fresh start with Jesus or have never followed Him, He waits for you.

> What does repentance mean? It means to change—to change your mind, change the way that you're living—and to determine that with God's help you will live for Christ.[17]

---

[16] James Strong, *The New Strong's Exhaustive Concordance of the Bible* (Nashville, TN: Thomas Nelson, 1995).

[17] Franklin Graham, *Billy Graham in Quotes* (Nashville, TN: Thomas Nelson, 2011).

Reflection

1. Have you accepted the key to heaven that Christ offers? You need only to repent and believe this very moment. Begin with Him now and live for Him always.

2. For more insight, read Luke 24:27, Acts 3:19, and Ephesians 2:8–9.

Prayer

Dear Savior,

You are the "Consolation of Israel" and the consolation of my heart. This very moment I *meanoiete* and *pisteuó*. You hold the keys to eternity, and I accept them now. With Your help, I will live for You!

Amen

#11

Exousia

I want you to know that the Son of Man
has authority on earth.
Matthew 9:6 (GW)

He is the radiance of the glory of God
and the exact imprint of his nature, and he upholds
the universe by the word of his power.
Hebrews 1:3 (ESV)

Exousia (Greek):
Power, authority, right, liberty, jurisdiction, strength[18]

Time and again, people were struck with wide-eyed amazement by the *exousia* of Jesus: when He chose and called His disciples, raised the dead, healed the sick, led His followers, preached with power, and cast out evil. This carpenter-turned-rabbi spoke with crazy conviction, even to the religious leaders. Once, He called them snakes and a brood of vipers. *Scandalous.*

So where did Christ get His clout, and how did He establish it? The Bible tells us that His Father gave it to Him:

---

[18] James Strong, *The New Strong's Exhaustive Concordance of the Bible* (Nashville, TN: Thomas Nelson, 1995).

- "You are my beloved Son." (Mark 1:11 ESV)
- "All things have been committed to me by my Father." (Matthew 11:27)
- "He has given him authority to judge because he is the Son of Man." (John 5:27)

Like the Hebrew crowds of old, I too stand in wide-eyed amazement at this carpenter-turned-rabbi who walked out His influence by doing what He was put on earth to do. And when we peel away the layers of His actions, we find a core of love. Love is the bottom line of everything the Son of God has ever done and ever will do for us. Through His Father, love was His authority. And in keeping with the Creator's plan, the torch was passed to us, the church of Christ.

We are anointed by the Lord to:

- Be called children of God (John 1:12)
- Approach the throne of grace with confidence (Hebrews 4:16)
- Preach the gospel of truth (Mark 16:15)
- Appeal to the world on Christ's behalf as His ambassadors (2 Corinthians 5:20)

Love is *our* authority.

When self-talk shouts out negative words about who I am, I open my ears to my heavenly Father's words and hear Him call me His child. When I perceive a barrier between the Maker of the world and me, I read that I have access to Him no matter what I've done, no matter where I am. When I feel inadequate to share the truth of the gospel with others, I remember that I am called to do so. When I find myself thinking that my life is an insignificant Christian example, I recall that because of Jesus's righteousness, the righteousness of God fills me, and I am worthy to stand up for Him.

This is true for everyone who has chosen Jesus, the supreme and scandalous Son of God, the one given clout by God, by decree from the throne of grace.

I Sing the Mighty Power of God

There's not a plant or flower below,
But makes Thy glories known;
And clouds arise, and tempests blow
By order from Thy throne.[19]

Reflection

1. Journal your thoughts on the Scriptures listed above.

2. As you read those passages, consider with wide-eyed amazement the *exousia* of Christ.

Prayer

Dear Savior,

You are the carpenter-turned-rabbi-turned-Savior. And because of this, I stand with my mouth agape, eyes wide in amazement, and hands lifted high. Because of You, I have authority to tell the world of God's love and to stand for Him. Thank You.

Amen

---

19   Isaac Watts, "I Sing the Mighty Power of God," 1907.

#12

His Language

On hearing this, Jesus said, "It is not the healthy
who need a doctor, but the sick. But go and learn
what this means: 'I desire mercy, not sacrifice.'
For I have not come to call the righteous, but sinners."
Matthew 9:12–13

My sister and I have a secret language; we call it Double-Talk.
As girls, we loved to exasperate our parents and talk about them
(and others) as we sat in the same room and they could not
understand us. Eventually, our husbands and kids felt the same
annoyance. It's a great party trick! The inside scoop on this secret
code (please don't tell anyone) is that we use actual English
words but mix them up in a pattern and speak them quickly. Jeni
and I get it, but it is too fast for the listener to parse what we are
saying.

It might seem silly to compare our Double-Talk with the
words of the Savior. However, sometimes when I read a Scripture
about people's confused reactions to His words, I picture the
faces of friends and family trying to figure out what Jeni and I are
saying. I imagine the Christ-listeners walking away, scratching
their heads, and saying, "Huh?" To the individuals around Him,
it might have sounded like Jesus spoke His own language. And

indeed, He did, because His message was radically perplexing, unlike anything ever heard before.

There are numerous passages of Scripture where Christ's followers and enemies did not understand the meaning of His words. The following two groups repeatedly misinterpreted the words of Jesus:

- His disciples (See Matthew 16:5–12, John 4:31–34, and John 14:1–11)
- His opponents (See John 2:19–21, John 6:31–33, and John 7:27–29)

In our key verse today, we read that after the Pharisees questioned the disciples, the Savior encouraged His followers to "go and learn." He desired that they know the truth for themselves, to think for themselves. Beyond this, Jesus promised to remedy the situation by sending the Holy Spirit (John 14:15–17). This promise is for those who love and obey His commands. This advocate, this Spirit of truth, will be with His followers forever, providing insight, power, and truth. The result is an inner transformation, giving believers a more complete comprehension of His communication. After the disciples received the Spirit of truth in Acts, the gaps filled where the men had failed to grasp His meanings.

Even though the Bible is not a secret language like the Double-Talk my sister and I used, there is much I don't understand. I love a good study Bible to help me heed Jesus's words to "go and learn." I like to read different translations to help bring clarity and illumination.

I believe we won't fully comprehend the Messiah's message until we meet Him face-to-face. Yet I do know that the same Holy Spirit who blew into the disciples at Pentecost is also a gift for you and me. He lives in the heart of all Christ-followers. The mystery of the Holy Spirit is just that: a mystery. However, the apostle Paul wrote that the Holy Spirit helps us in our weakness (Romans 8:26), and *that* I understand.

> The Helper (Comforter, Advocate, Intercessor—Counselor, Strengthener, Standby), the Holy Spirit, whom the Father will send in My name [in My place, to represent Me and act on My behalf], He will teach you all things. And He will help you remember everything that I have told you.
> John 14:26 (AMP)

Reflection

1. Do you usually understand the language of Christ when you read the Gospels? Or is it a mystery to you?

2. Read the story of Pentecost in Acts chapter 2. Record your thoughts.

Prayer
Dear Savior,

I pray for continued wisdom and understanding as I read Your Word. Thank You for Your promise of the Holy Spirit, who will teach me and help me remember all that You have told me as I "go and learn."

Amen

#13

Do You Want to Get Well?

When Jesus saw him lying there and learned
that he had been in this condition for a long time,
he asked him, "Do you want to get well?"
John 5:6

Hundreds of people—blind, sick, and paralyzed—waited by the healing waters of Bethsaida in Jerusalem. Some under porches erected so the masses could wait in the shade. It was believed that the first to enter the moving water early in the day would be healed.

"Do you want to get well?"

On a sunny Sabbath morning, Jesus strode through the porches. He directed His gaze to a man lying on a mat who had been crippled for thirty-eight years. Our Savior gently asked him a question with what seemed like an obvious answer. Instead of a hearty, "Yes!" the man replied, "I have no one to help me into the pool when the water is stirred. While I am trying to get in, someone else goes down ahead of me" (John 5:7).

Thirty-eight years and that is his answer? Some people can be downright comfy in their sickness, unable to move forward, if they are looking back. It becomes part of their identity, a way to garner attention. One of my family members spent a lifetime looking for attention through illness and infirmity. It could be that some do not want to get well because their pain serves as a salve to their emotional ruins.

"Do you want to get well?"

Christ did not coddle the crippled. He wasted no time in His response to the man by the pool. "Then Jesus said to him, 'Get up! Pick up your mat and walk'" (John 5:8).

Immediately the man was well and walking.

Sometimes we take our time before doing what we know is best—before we do what God asks us. We overthink and underdo.

The Healer required the lame man to obey right away, with no more thought to his illness or excuses. Is He expecting the same of us in our current condition? Perhaps it is time to jump up and get on with it.

"Do you want to get well?"

Let's fast-forward this story to a second interaction between the Son of God and the crippled man in John 5:14. "Later Jesus found him at the temple and said to him, 'See, you are well again. Stop sinning or something worse may happen to you.'"

Is there insight here into why the man was ill? Was his paralysis related to his past sin? Did he jump back into his vices as soon as he could walk? Or maybe he was too comfortable in his sin to want true healing of body *and* soul.

Followers of Christ are given the gift of wholeness of spirit. Like the lame man, this gift is offered without any merit or deserving on our part. And, like the man with the mat, we too need to be reminded to stop sinning, to keep a check on our soul, or there will be consequences.

We are all helpless and weak and crippled in some way, waiting by the pool of Bethsaida. Today we can reach out for the renewing and healing touch of the Messiah. His gentle reminder tells us to be well, to live for Him, and to stop sinning. Authentically healed and whole.

> Praise the Lord, my soul,
> and forget not all his benefits—
> who forgives all your sins
> and heals all your diseases.
> Psalm 103:2–3

Reflection

1. Read the entirety of John 5:1–18. Record your thoughts.

2. Do you see yourself in the lame man? If so, do you need spiritual or physical healing (or both)? Do you need to turn from your sin?

Prayer

Dear Savior,

I picture myself next to this man and the multitude of others lying by the pool and under the porches waiting for healing. At this moment, I listen for Your voice that says to me, "Get up and pick up your mat and walk!" So today, I chose to do so and live for You. I want to be well.

Amen

#14

Kinsman-Redeemer

Today this scripture is fulfilled in your hearing.
Luke 4:21

Nazareth. The village where Jesus grew up. A tight-knit community where many people were kin to Christ. They had watched Him grow from a little boy to become a common carpenter. A normal guy from a normal family from a normal town.

I find it interesting that Christ did not begin His public ministry in Nazareth. After the forty-day temptation from Satan, He chose to start in Capernaum, on the shores of the Sea of Galilee. After He made a splash there and traveled widely in that region, He strode on the familiar hills of His native soil with authority and power never expressed there before.

Once home, He went to the synagogue to read from the Scriptures, as was the norm. The people of Nazareth had heard the marvelous stories of their kinsman, but I imagine they questioned those stories and His lifestyle. Why did He leave them to live on the road as a self-appointed rabbi and teacher? Was He a prophet? As they curiously settled in to listen, Christ stood in the front of the room, all eyes on Him.

He unrolled the scroll and read from Isaiah:

The Spirit of the Lord is on me,
because he has anointed me
to proclaim good news to the poor.
He has sent me to proclaim freedom for the prisoners
and recovery of sight for the blind,
to set the oppressed free,
to proclaim the year of the Lord's favor.
Luke 4:18–19

Here's where it gets wild. After He rolled up the scroll, He sat down and told these familiar folks in His familiar church that this familiar Scripture He had just recited was fulfilled in their hearing.

By Him.

Wait. Say what?

Look how The Message translation puts it in verse 22: "All who were there, watching and listening, were surprised at how well he spoke. But they also said, 'Isn't this Joseph's son, the one we've known since he was just a kid?'"

What they could not see or would not see was that Joseph's son was not a prophet or a super-smart, well-spoken rabbi. He was their long-awaited Messiah, the fulfillment of prophecy. Their Kinsman-Redeemer.

A kinsman-redeemer is a relative who redeems, protects, and gathers his loved ones to himself. This Jesus from Nazareth was one of their own, made like them, sent to deliver them. Yet they became increasingly enraged by His declarations and refused to accept Him as Messiah.

And what is even wilder than what happened that day in the synagogue is this truth: we too are His own. Hebrews 2:11 says that Christ is not ashamed to call us His brothers and sisters. We are His kin; He is our Kinsman-Redeemer. The fulfillment of a line of love from generation to generation to us today.

Therefore, it was necessary for him to be made in every respect like us, his brothers and sisters, so that he could be our merciful and faithful High Priest before God. Then he could offer a sacrifice that would take away the sins of the people.

Hebrews 2:17 (NLT)

Reflection

1. Read Luke 4:18–19 aloud and substitute the word "me" for "Jesus Christ."

2. For a beautiful depiction of a kinsman-redeemer, read the book of Ruth.

Prayer

Dear Savior,

I stand amazed. You are the fulfillment of prophecy, the Kinsman-Redeemer, and a line of love through generations. Thank You for gathering me to You and making me Your own.

Amen

#15
A City on a Hill

You are the light of the world. A city set on a hill.
Matthew 5:14 (NASB)

The Sermon on the Mount—this eloquent, instructive, and convicting discourse from our Savior—is found in Matthew chapters 5 through 7. Here Jesus explains what it means to follow Him in God's kingdom. If this is not a familiar passage to you (or even if it is), I encourage you to read it all.

Enormous, curious crowds gathered at each place the Messiah stopped. He was at the pinnacle of His popularity. Sometimes, instead of speaking to the masses, the Savior would move to a private place to sit intimately with His disciples. And this is what He did on the day of His now-famous Sermon on the Mount. "One day as he saw the crowds gathering, Jesus went up on the mountainside and sat down. His disciples gathered around him, and he began to teach them" (Matthew 5:1–2 NLT).

On a grassy hillside by the Sea of Galilee, one of the lessons the Messiah imparted to His men was that they were to be a light. Not just a barely burning candle but the light of the world and a city on a hill.

Many cities in Judea were built on the sides of mountains and could be seen over a widespread region. Therefore, the metaphor made sense to the men listening. Perhaps they could see such a city from where they sat.

I wonder what pictures formed in the minds of this motley group of men sitting in the tall grass. How did they respond to their rabbi after hearing His vision for them? How could they have imagined the radical fire beam of light their small circle would shine on the future of the world?

Like those early disciples, you and I also belong to a body of believers whom God created to glow like a luminous flame on a moonless night. A city on a hill. In our modern world, we have an opportunity to radiate as one for Jesus as never before. Perhaps in a community that feeds the needy. Or in a church that supplies clothes and school supplies to poor students. The opportunities abound! I find myself hope-filled and compelled by these words of the Savior to join fellow Christ-followers as we shine collectively.

I am also determined to be a light bearer for my Savior individually in my little world. Jesus goes on to say, "In the same way, let your light shine before others, that they may see your good deeds and glorify your Father in heaven" (Matthew 5:16).

This Scripture inspires me in His calling for me to shimmer and serve on my own hill. As children of the King, we can reflect His radiant love to those He puts on our paths. Hurting souls in desperate need of hope in an often lonely, difficult world. Those who need a friend, a hug, or a meal.

"This little light of mine, I'm gonna let it shine."[20]

In him was life, and that life was the light of all mankind.
The light shines in the darkness,
and the darkness has not overcome it.
John 1:4–5

---

[20]   John Avery Lomax, "This Little Light of Mine," 1939.

Reflection

1. Where and how do you want to shine collectively for Christ? Is it time to join a group or a church?

2. How about on your own hill? As an individual, what practical ways might you shine for Him this Easter?

Prayer

Dear Savior,

I invite Your light to sparkle brightly inside me today as I walk collectively and individually as Your follower. Shine through me each day of this Easter season and beyond!

Amen

#16

Fulfilled and New

Do not think that I have come to abolish the Law
or the Prophets; I have not come to abolish them
but to fulfill them.
Matthew 5:17

ἐπιτελέω / *epileléō* (verb):
Complete, accomplish, perfect[21]

From His mountain pulpit, our Savior shared with His followers a shocking declaration when He voiced His objective in coming to live and die on earth.

Interestingly, He said first what He did *not* come to do. He made it clear that His intent was not to eliminate the Law and the Prophets, and it seems this was something not to be misunderstood.

Jesus then went on to tell them what He *did* come to do. He intended to fulfill the prophets' words and make the law whole. These prophet predictions about the coming Messiah in the Old Testament (there are hundreds of them) were realized in Christ

---

[21]   *New Testament Greek Lexicon*, Bible Tools, https://www.biblestudytools.com/lexicons/greek/kjv/epiteleo.html.

Jesus, the only one who could uphold the high standard of the law's regulations.

Hebrews 10 tells us that because of this fulfillment, priests would no longer be required to enter the holy place to offer sacrifices to God for the sins of imperfect people like you and me. Jesus replaced this requirement when He obtained our eternal salvation and made us right with God by His death on the cross.

The Savior's sacrificial death on Calvary's hill, and His subsequent resurrection three days later, presented a permanent and perfect sacrifice on our behalf.

This outrageous man, sitting on a mountain surrounded by listeners in rapt attention, told them He came to finish the Old Covenant with its thousands of rules and restrictions. He came to establish a New Covenant. He was the *very* one the prophets had foretold.

More shocking words had never been spoken. The law began with Moses on another mount, called Sinai. It was the air the Jews breathed and the noose the priests placed around their collective neck. Hebrews 7:22 (ESV) explains, "This makes Jesus the guarantor of a better covenant."

A better one!

Under the New Covenant:

- We have the gift of salvation. (Ephesians 2:8–9)
- We are made new. (2 Corinthians 5:17)
- We are free, not bound to the old ways. (Galatians 5:1)
- We are filled with the Holy Spirit. (Romans 8:9–11)
- We live under grace, not law. (Romans 6:14)
- We have a perpetual and permanent relationship with God. (Hebrews 9:15)
- *All* are welcome to come to God, not just the Jews. (Acts 15:19)

This controversial Christ and His shocking fulfillments were a present from the God of the universe for the Jews of Jesus's day to unwrap. This fresh covenant gift was tied with a beautiful bow called *freedom*. Freedom from sin, from death, from legality ... and so much more.

This gift is for us too. The message of the end of the old and the start of the miraculous new is for every disciple from that day on the mountain to us today.

> The Torah (law of Moses at Sinai) is given for a specific period of time and is then set aside—not because it was a bad thing now happily abolished, but because it was a good thing whose purpose had been accomplished.[22]

Reflection

1. Read and consider the following Scriptures regarding Christ's fulfilled prophecy: Matthew 1:22–23, Matthew 13:34–35, and John 19:36.

2. How do the Old and New Covenants apply to us today? (See Galatians 3:23–29.)

---

[22] N. T. Wright, *The Climax of the Covenant: Christ and the Law in Pauline Theology* (Minneapolis, MN: Fortress Press, 1993).

Prayer

Dear Savior,

Thank You for completing the Law and the Prophets. For making all things new. For Your astonishing gift of freedom proclaimed in the Sermon on the Mount.

Amen

#17

Fight for It!

Jesus turned around, and when he saw her he said,
"Daughter, be encouraged! Your faith has made you well."
And the woman was healed at that moment.
Matthew 9:22 (NLT)

We don't know her name, but she is the only woman Jesus ever referred to as "daughter."

I think she should be called "The Woman Who Fought for It."

She was prohibited from touching anyone, considered unclean due to a condition that had afflicted her for twelve years. She used all her money to visit healers who offered no cure for her illness. Even still, she possessed a tenacious faith. "She said within herself, if I may but touch his garment, I shall be whole" (Matthew 9:21 WBT).

As an animated throng swarmed around the Savior, this woman pushed past her fears and cultural conventions and grasped the tassel of the Healer's cloak.

And healed she was.

I see echoes of myself in this woman. (How I wish we knew her name!) My journey has been strewn with one painful, draining condition to the next. And not all physical. There is a slew of emotional afflictions painted on my life's canvas.

This portrait of pain began in early childhood, and as I retrace those moments, my heart feels the emotions all over again. I am grateful that the paintbrush also rendered many cheerful colors along the way, but the blacks and grays are consistent in the mix. I felt downright wrecked at times, as if my soul were broken.

But God. My God has shown me beauty in my brokenness.

You see, when we flip the fallout and allow ourselves to view our brokenness with a divine lens, our perspective shifts as we discover the fingers of God holding the paintbrush. This requires a tenacious faith, as the woman in Matthew 9 displayed. Such a daring move by this long-suffering believer. This fighter.

We too must fight to be whole.

I battle for wholeness and health most days, and it is hard. It does not come naturally for me. But I set an intention years ago to work through some wreckage that was still wrecking me. To fight for my health. One day at a time, I put on my divine lens and fight my way to wellness. I hold fast to the tassel on Jesus's cloak and pray as God paints my pain with His purposes and says to me, "Daughter, be encouraged. Your faith has made you well."

My friend, it is worth the work. Jesus wants you whole in Him. So today, dare to touch the hem of His garment and be encouraged. May your faith make you well as you fight for it!

Only one person was commended that day for having faith. It wasn't a wealthy giver. It wasn't a loyal follower. It was a shame-struck, penniless outcast who clutched onto her hunch that He could help and her hope that He would.[23]

---

23   Max Lucado, *Jesus: The God Who Knows Your Name* (Nashville, TN: Thomas Nelson, 2020), 112.

Reflection

1. When has God come to you in a broken place? Write your thoughts as a prayer of thanks.

2. In what ways do you see echoes of yourself in this woman?

Prayer

Dear Savior,

I yield my beautifully broken soul to You. This Easter season, I will fight for healing and hold tightly to the hem of Your garment. Thank You for the story of this tenacious daughter of faith whose name You know oh so well.

Amen

#18

I Have a Question for You

Jesus said to his critics, "I have a question for you.
Does the law permit good deeds on the Sabbath,
or is it a day for doing evil? Is this a day to save life
or to destroy it?"
Luke 6:9 (NLT)

It was still early in Jesus's ministry, but the lines were already drawn. The religious leaders scrutinized this different kind of rabbi, looking for a reason to accuse Him, especially when each Sabbath day came around. In Jewish legal tradition, thirty-nine classifications of activities were not allowed on the Sabbath, and healing was one of them. Healing was considered the practice of medicine, and Jews could not practice their professions on the Sabbath.

As Christ taught in the synagogue one Sabbath day, a man with a crippled hand sat watching and listening to the Teacher. As did the suspicious Pharisees and teachers of the law, ready to pounce if Christ chose to break their rules. Some scholars believe the leaders planted the crippled man as a setup. Jesus knew the thoughts and intentions moving through the minds of the Pharisees. In challenging them, the Messiah drew out their faulty motives and unjust interpretation of the law for all to see. These callous men cared more about making a mockery of Christ than seeing a crippled man made well.

Even during His anger toward them, Jesus grieved for their hardness and hypocrisy. Mark 3:5 (NLT) says, "He looked around at them angrily and was deeply saddened by their hard hearts." He knew His future. He knew these same people would be responsible for His death.

I find myself irked as I read this passage. How dare these men go after Christ as they did! Yet are they so different from me?

These religious men were born and raised and primed for this life. It was all they knew. They loved to swim in their notoriety and high positions in the community, so much so that their focus became clouded. They lost sight of their purpose, which was to point people toward the Lord. Out of all of society, these religious men should have recognized the Messiah. Instead, they could not see Him for who He was because He threatened their position and power and egos.

Would I have done the same?

Jesus called the man with the withered hand to stand. As the two men faced both the crowd and the Pharisees, Jesus asked a probing question. "Let me ask you something: What kind of action suits the Sabbath best? Doing good or doing evil? Helping people or leaving them helpless?" (Luke 6:9 MSG).

When no one answered His question, Christ told the man to stretch out his hand. As he did so, he became healed. Interestingly, because Christ did not set a bone or perform surgery, no profession was practiced. Therefore, this healing on the Sabbath did not violate God's law, only the Pharisees' interpretation of the law. These men, so hindered by hatred and jealousy, did not see their inconsistent and unclear opposition to Christ's actions.

The Bible does not say how the crowd in the synagogue responded, but I imagine there was a collective gasp. The air inside was awash with challenge and change; there would be no undrawing of the lines. From this moment forward, these incensed religious leaders began to plot Christ's death.

And murder was an act absolutely against the law.

By this novel way of putting His case, our Lord teaches the great ethical principle, that to neglect any opportunity of doing good is to incur the guilt of doing evil; and by this law He bound His own spirit.[24]

Reflection

1. Luke 11:37–44 is a powerful section of Scripture where Jesus criticizes the Pharisees. Read this passage and record your thoughts.

2. Imagine yourself in Christ's day as a Pharisee or religious teacher, prepared for such a life from infancy. How do you believe you would have responded when Christ came on the scene?

---

[24] Robert Jamieson, A. R. Fausset, and David Brown, *Jamieson, Fausset, and Brown's Commentary on the Whole Bible* (Grand Rapids, MI: Zondervan, 1979).

Prayer

Dear Savior,

I sit before You now and confess any pharisaical tendencies that may be hiding in my heart and for the times my ego gets in the way. I thank You for creating the Sabbath for people, not people for the Sabbath. In Your eyes, any day is the right day to do good. May I do good for others every day.

Amen

#19

Precious in His Sight

Let the little children come to Me, and do not forbid
them; for of such is the kingdom of God. Assuredly,
I say to you, whoever does not receive the kingdom
of God as a little child will by no means enter it.
Mark 10:14–15 (NKJV)

In my childhood home, on the bottom of an end table sat a Bible story picture book. I still own this precious possession with its taped-up spine. It is filled with beautiful illustrations of deep contrasting colors and tones. As I curled up to read, my small fingers often turned to the story of Jesus and the children from Mark 10. I saw delight on the face of God's Son, and my heart attached itself to this kind Savior. His smile radiated with love for the little ones, so precious in His sight, as He held them on His lap.

In this tender scene, Christ messed with cultural conventions.

The disciples looked on, red-faced, as mothers and fathers brought their offspring to the rabbi for a touch of blessing. They rebuked and scolded the parents.

Children were regarded differently in the first century than they are today in Western culture. Since they did not contribute but instead took away from a family's finances, they were considered insignificant and ranked low on the societal scale. No power. No importance. In the eyes of the disciples, their leader was giving too much of Himself to those tiny, trivial people.

The Message translates Christ's response to His disciples this way: "Jesus was irate and let them know it: 'Don't push these children away. Don't ever get between them and me. These children are at the very center of life in the kingdom'" (Mark 10:14–15).

Jesus created analogies using children to illustrate our relationship with God, the realities of faith, grace, and the kingdom. His words and actions melded together to paint a potent picture when He said we must come to Him as little children.

Considering this, let's ask: *Who were the people the Messiah deemed valuable and significant?* My Bible storybook illuminates our answer in page after page of vibrant color: the outcasts, the sick, the sinners, the powerless, the rich, the poor, the least. All humankind.

Now let's personalize this portrait and ask: *Who are the people I deem valuable to me, and who are those least important?* How can I flip the cultural script as Jesus did and seek out the least, those with seemingly no power or importance in the social order?

As Christ-followers, each of us is a representation of Him. Even if we fumble at times, we are charged to bear His image as we love and do for those who are precious in His sight.

Jesus Loves the Little Children

Jesus loves the little children,
All the children of the world;
Red and yellow, black and white,
They are precious in His sight,
Jesus loves the little children of the world.[25]

---

[25]   Clarence Herbert Woolston, "Jesus Loves the Little Children," 1864.

Reflection

1. Read the following Scriptures, each comparing children to those who believe in Christ: Luke 10:21, Galatians 4:19, and 1 John 4:4.

2. Think about your community. Choose a person or a group with "no power" whom you may serve this Easter season.

Prayer

Dear Savior,

As You hold out Your arms, I run to You. As I climb onto Your lap, my eyes take in others around us. There is diversity in age, color, status, and reputation. Your eyes shine with adoration as You hold us close. *All* of us. Thank You, my Jesus, that my heart is forever attached to Yours.

Amen

#20

Ears to Hear

Jesus said, "Whoever has ears to hear, let them hear."
Mark 4:9

Parable (*parabolé*, Greek):
Illustrative comparison[26]

Years ago, in the margin of my Bible next to today's Scripture in Mark, I wrote in bold letters, "Do I have ears to hear?" It is a question worthy of thought. How much of Jesus's words do I "hear" when I read the Gospels? How much do I gloss over without genuinely attending to what God has for me? How often do I allow my phone or other distractions to divert me from the depth of His message?

I encourage you to read the parable of the soils (also called the parable of the sower) in Mark 4:1–25. Today let's touch on a few notable points.

Christ loved to teach in parables. Altogether, thirty-eight of these stories are told in three out of the four Gospels (none in the book of John). A parable often uses ordinary images and situations familiar to the listeners to illustrate a bigger truth.

---

[26] James Strong, *The New Strong's Exhaustive Concordance of the Bible* (Nashville, TN: Thomas Nelson, 1995).

Jesus sat in a boat near the shore outside Capernaum. Enormous crowds gathered around, standing close to the water's edge, all eyes trained on Him. Before He began to teach, He voiced a command: "Listen to this!" (verse 3 NASB)

In this parable, Jesus taught that sometimes seeds would scatter and land in spots where they could not grow. The people listened as Jesus told of the outcome of the seed based on where it landed in four different scenarios. As He ended His illustration, He circled back to this key concept of listening. The Message puts verse 9 this way: "Are you listening to this? Really listening?"

The parable of the soils contrasts different kinds of hearers. Those with "ears to hear" allow God's words to take seed in them and bear fruit for His purposes. When Jesus spoke to those who have ears, He referred to all who had heard His words. Yet there is a distinction between having ears and having "ears to hear."

After the crowds drifted off, Mark lets us eavesdrop on an exchange between Jesus and the disciples. The men were confused by the meaning of the story. Christ's warning in verse 13 is significant. He said they would not understand *any* of His parables unless they heard and comprehended the importance of the lesson. Again Jesus brought home the vital concept of listening. He referenced Isaiah 6, which speaks of people who have eyes and ears yet who have hardened their hearts and chosen to ignore the word of the Lord. He wanted the disciples to have ears to hear, unlike the crowds who flitted off when they didn't like the message or found something or someone more entertaining.

Just like us, with our modern-day technology and distractions. These distractions aren't all bad, of course. Yet unless we are ready to tune out diversions and come to Jesus to understand the meaning of His preaching, His words will only be empty stories. We need more than ears; we need ears to hear.

In the years since I wrote that question in my Bible, I have learned that hearing God's truth takes energy and focus; it takes a willingness to be challenged and changed. It takes ears to hear. This parable is as poignant to me today as it was then because I know the way of God's truth is not always convenient or fun. Yet now more than ever, I desire for His seed to land in the fertile ground of my heart and for His purpose to be fulfilled in me.

> "Keep on hearing, but do not understand;
> keep on seeing, but do not perceive."
> Make the heart of this people dull,
> and their ears heavy,
> and blind their eyes;
> lest they see with their eyes,
> and hear with their ears,
> and understand with their hearts,
> and turn and be healed.
> Isaiah 6:9–10 (ESV)

Reflection

1. For further study, read Matthew 7:24–27, John 10:27–28, Revelation 2:7, Revelation 3:20, and Revelation 13:9.

2. Do you have ears to hear?

Prayer

Dear Savior,

Give me ears to hear! Thank You for the wisdom in the parable of the soils. I pray Your seed will land in the fertile ground of my heart. May Your purpose be fulfilled in me.

Amen

#21

Room for Rest

The apostles gathered around Jesus and reported to him
all they had done and taught. Then, because so many
people were coming and going that they did not even
have a chance to eat, he said to them, "Come with me by
yourselves to a quiet place and get some rest."
Mark 6:30–31

This season, I am looking at Lent differently than I have in the past. Many in the Christian faith choose to observe Lent by fasting from something (meat, sugar, TV, social media) in the weeks approaching Easter. I have often done the same. But this year I have chosen to fast from my "to do" list. I am making room for rest, exchanging busyness for time in quiet contemplation.

I am weary. As I write, I am recovering from an illness that has gripped me for six months. I am learning to accept what my body can and cannot do, build margins around my health, and allow others to pick up my slack. I don't like it, yet invincible I am not. So I lean in. I transfer trust in my strength to my Savior's.

In God's Word, we read how the Messiah repeatedly made room for rest; it was a priority in His ministry. He took His men away from the expectant, demanding masses to recharge, and He often got away by Himself.

We find an example of this in Mark chapter 6. Jesus sent the disciples out two by two to minister to the people of Galilee. He gave them His divine authority to preach, heal, and cast out demons. They returned to Him with accounts of their triumphs and the stories of God's achievements. The crowds clamored to get to the Master and His men, who needed rest and care after a busy time. So the Savior insisted they steal away together to refocus, recover, sabbath, and spend intimate time as a group.

I love that Christ implores us in His Word to come to Him for rest. "Come to me, all you who are weary and burdened, and I will give you rest" (Matthew 11:28). It's like a holy permission slip. In fact, Jesus called Himself the Lord of the Sabbath in Matthew 12:8.

Hebrews 4:9–10 says, "There remains, then, a Sabbath-rest for the people of God; for anyone who enters God's rest also rests from their works, just as God did from his." This Lenten season is the perfect time for us, the people of God, to take as much off the to-do list as possible, follow the Savior's example, and cease striving. Let us sit at His feet and fix our eyes and hearts closer than we ever have before on His death and resurrection.

Let us lean into God's Sabbath rest.

To enter our Sabbath rest, we must come to God in humble submission to His truth and in complete dependence on Him. In order to cease striving, we must transfer our trust away from our own abilities, our own accomplishments, our own strength, and place it on His provisions.[27]

Reflection

---

[27] Charles R. Swindoll, *Great Lives: Jesus: The Greatest Life of All* (Nashville, TN: Thomas Nelson, 2009).

1. Are you weary? Do you need to cease striving and take some things off your to-do list?

2. Write down ways you will build margin in your life this Lenten season.

Prayer

Dear Savior,

I sit before You in quiet contemplation. I choose to build margin and rest into these weeks of Lent. As I fix my eyes and heart on You, I release the hurry and trust You with everything I think I need to do.

Amen

#22

Do You Want to Leave Too?

From that time on many of His disciples turned back and
no longer walked with Him. So Jesus asked the Twelve,
"Do you want to leave too?"
Simon Peter replied, "Lord, to whom would we go? You
have the words of eternal life. We believe and know that
You are the Holy One of God."
John 6:66–69 (BSB)

Many of Jesus's followers were defecting, and He faced pushback
from the Jewish leaders on His tough-to-swallow truths. Jesus
claimed to be the Bread of Life, sent from heaven. Some of His
devotees began to mutter and question His validity. The word on
the street was that He was *not* from heaven, just a crazy carpenter.
After many He had taught, healed, and loved into light turned
away, the Messiah gazed deeply into the eyes of the Twelve. He
then asked them if they too wanted to leave.

The intensity of this moment moves me as I picture Peter's face.
Perhaps tears spilled as he looked squarely at his Savior. Peter's
reply—"To whom would we go?"—was not really a question but

a declaration. Peter wasn't asking Jesus to name someone else for the Twelve to follow. He was saying there *was* no one else.

Peter's statement is profound. This is my favorite response to Jesus in all the Gospels, because I too have uttered it in times when I was in a dark pit of doubt.

To whom would they go? No one could replace Jesus. He was their Teacher (Matthew 4:23), their Way (John 14:6), their Shepherd (John 10:11), their friend (John 15:13), and their God (John 20:28). They had given their lives to His call.

Never has a spiritual teacher or philosopher claimed the same message as the man from Nazareth. Not Gandhi, Buddha, Krishna, Mohammed, or even Moses. The Messiah alone holds the power of eternal life. The Message puts Peter's next words this way: "You have the words of real life, eternal life. We've already committed ourselves, confident that you are the Holy One of God" (John 6:68). After His Savior ascended to heaven, Peter went on to preach these words: "There is salvation in no one else! God has given no other name under heaven by which we must be saved" (Acts 4:12 NLT).

No other name.

How about you and me? Where else would *we* go?

Maybe you find yourself in a pit of doubt. Perhaps there are profound disappointments in your life that hang on. *And on.* Are there prayers that go unanswered? Loved ones who've walked away from their faith? Sometimes the narrow path is lonely, and His truths are tough to swallow. Jesus can feel so far away.

Here in these hard places, I remind myself that He is my Teacher, my Way, my Shepherd, my best friend, and my God. And so much more. No one offers what He offers and gives what He gives. Even when He seems far away and the road is rough, I choose Him. I give my life to His call. I follow His path, knowing, as the disciples did, that He will never leave or forsake me.

Friend, until we stand in His holy presence and see Him face-to-face, let us journey close to Him this Easter time as never before. Where else would we go?

> Blessed are those who understand what is afoot
> and stay on My narrow path.
> Matthew 11:6 (VOICE)

Reflection

1. Have you ever followed or been tempted to follow a leader or philosophy other than Jesus and His way?

2. In moments of doubt, where do you go? What do you do?

Prayer

Dear Savior,

I acknowledge my moments of doubt and disbelief, the dark moments where I feel as if I am in a pit. I know even when I don't feel You, You are with me. There is nowhere else I want to go; no one else will satisfy me. Thank You for never leaving or forsaking me.

Amen

#23

Who Do You Say I Am?

When Jesus came to the region of Caesarea Philippi,
he asked his disciples, "Who do people say
that the Son of Man is?"
"Well," they replied, "some say John the Baptist,
some say Elijah, and others say Jeremiah
or one of the other prophets."
Then he asked them, "But who do you say I am?"
Matthew 16:13–15 (NLT)

Hawaii disappeared from the plane's window—our trip was coming to an end. I sat on the plane, the echo of our laughter and adventures falling behind, and I felt a growing hollowness. Even though the college girls' trip to Hawaii had been a blast, I felt an inner void on our return. My life was filled with fun but lacked depth. I had stopped reading my Bible and attending church, and I kept my Christian friends at a distance.

I examined my life as I gazed at the clouds from the airplane window. I thought of my purpose, my future, the way I spent my time, and my relationship with Jesus. Who was He to me? Tears escaped while I timidly began to pray. This wasn't something I did much of in those days. As I confessed my emptiness, a gentle whisper flowed through my heart. *Who do you say I am?*

The most important question.

In Matthew 16, the disciples shared with their leader the common view of who people said He was: John the Baptist or Elijah or a prophet. Varied responses like the ones we still hear today: an imposter, a crazy man, a good teacher, the Savior.

Then Jesus turned the inquiry to them, His beloved Twelve. Peter, ever impassioned, spoke up immediately. "You are the Messiah, the Son of the living God" (Matthew 16:16 NLT). Peter was right, although this Son of God was not what they expected Him to be.

From this point on, Christ began to open the shades, shining specks of light on His future as the suffering King. He preached on themes from the prophet Isaiah and probed the Twelve along the way.

This same query asked in the intimacy of this group in Caesarea rumbles down through the centuries to us in this moment.

The most important question leads to the most important answer.

My pensive prayers that day in an airplane's seat changed my life trajectory. It didn't happen immediately, though. After a year of wooing on God's part, tears gushed through choked words on a balmy summer evening on a San Diego freeway. On this brilliant sunset drive, I gave God my most important answer. I professed my need for Him as I replied to my soul's whisper, *You are the Savior. You are my Savior.*

The purpose of my life shifted and took shape the night I made my choice.

The Savior asks, "Who do you say I am?" Ultimately, each one of us must respond to this central question of life for ourselves. What we think of Him determines who we are and what we do, the trajectory of our lives on earth and for eternity.

Dear friend, who do *you* say He is?

> You must make your choice. Either this man was
> the Son of God, or else a madman or something worse.[28]

Reflection

1. How does the answer to this question determine how you live each day? In your journal, record who you think Jesus is.

2. Read what the Bible says about who He is: Messiah (Matthew 1:1), Savior of the world (1 John 4:14), and Word Incarnate (John 1:14–18). What do each of these titles mean to you?

Prayer

Dear Savior,

You are the Messiah, the Savior of the world, the Word Incarnate, and so much more! Help me to remember the truth of who You are, to believe this truth, and to live each day of Lent and beyond in light of the answer to the most important question.

Amen

---

[28] C. S. Lewis, *Mere Christianity* (San Francisco, CA: HarperOne, 2015).

#24

Give Up Your Own Way

Jesus said to his disciples,
"If any of you wants to be my follower, you must give up
your own way, take up your cross, and follow me."
Matthew 16:24 (NLT)

Jesus lounged in the sun with His twelve disciples on the pebbly shore of a blue-green lake called the Sea of Galilee. The conversation turned grave as Jesus predicted His death for the first time (Matthew 16:21). He then called out these men who had already given up so much—the comfort of home and family, the stability of steady work and income, their possessions, their reputation as "normal" Jewish men—as He told them that to truly follow Him, they would need to take up their crosses and give up their own way.

Before this day on the shore, other disciples left. Possibly tired of going the way of this man from Nazareth, weary of the travel, missing family and security. Perhaps they wondered why He had not become the powerful Messiah-King they had expected. "At this point many of his disciples turned away and deserted him. Then Jesus turned to the Twelve and asked, 'Are you also going to leave?'" (John 6:66–67 NLT).

But the Twelve remained.

These twelve understood Jesus's illustration of taking up their crosses to follow Him since Roman crucifixion was a common method of execution in their world. The Romans required the condemned to carry their crosses through the town until they arrived at their site of death. Jesus did not dance around His words in that lakeside moment. To go further with Him meant a costly commitment: the risk of death, and no turning back.

To follow Christ means pledging one's whole being to His service, with a great possibility of significant cost.

The cross is a depiction of death, surrender, sacrifice ... pain. Yet today we wear the beloved symbol of the Christian faith around our necks and hang it on the walls in our homes. Because more than death, this symbol we cherish is a sign of miraculous hope. This intersection of two pieces of wood illustrates the intersection of God's love: one piece reaches up as a reflection of His holiness, the other spreads across as an expression of the breadth of His love. This is the intersection of the gift of eternity.

The ones who stayed with Jesus found this hope worth it all. Found Jesus worth it all. Eventually, eleven of these apostles renounced all that remained of their own way and gave their lives for the Savior, martyred for their Messiah—two nailed to a cross.

What does it mean to give up our own way, right here, right now? Picture yourself sitting with your Savior on the lakeshore, a cross lying in the grass. What does He ask of you in this moment? Will you take up your cross and follow Him?

Take Up Thy Cross, the Savior Said

"Take up thy Cross," the Savior said,
"if thou wouldst my disciple be;

deny thyself, the world forsake,
and humbly follow after me."[29]

Reflection

1. What does it mean to you to pledge your life to Christ and to give up your own way?

2. Read Acts 12:1–4 and Hebrews 11:36–40. Journal your thoughts.

Prayer

Dear Savior,

Show me day by day what it means to take up my cross and live for You. In this quiet moment, I picture myself sitting in Your love under the shadow of the cross. I thank You that I have all of eternity before me because of Your sacrifice.

Amen

---

[29] Charles W. Everest, "Take Up Thy Cross, the Savior Said," 1833.

#25
What Is Your Mountain?

The disciples came to Jesus privately and said,
"Why could we not cast it out?"
And He said to them, "Because of your meager faith;
for truly I say to you, if you have faith the size
of a mustard seed, you will say to this mountain,
'Move from here to there,' and it will move;
and nothing will be impossible for you."
Matthew 17:19–20 (NASB)

I am not a fighter. I am a peacemaker. I want the people I love to live in peace with the people they love. I was born this way to a certain extent, but buried motives lurk behind my craving for harmony. Life scratched me up and tore at me. People disappointed, rejected, and betrayed me. Fear took root, spread its ugly tentacles, and became something I could keep covered if I dialed down the loud. The hard.

Along the way, I became a girl who labored to keep her environment calm and noncombative. As I mothered four rowdy, competitive boys, it became a never-ending battle and an impossible endeavor. When my marriage seemed lost and our financial situation dire, I developed a craving to control so the fear would not control me. Yet this tightrope of juggling fear and control made me oh so tired.

You might know a bit about this weary walk yourself.

In Matthew 17 we read of the disciples' confusion. They asked Jesus why He could drive a demon out of a boy and they could not. He said they hadn't enough faith and that even the smallest mustard seed of faith can move a mountain. Then in verse 20 Jesus added, "Nothing will be impossible for you."

Nothing. This bold statement from our Savior summons courage in me.

From a place of exhaustion, I recently confessed to Jesus that fear was my mountain, and it needed to move. In this place of pain and surrender, I wept as the God of love held my hands and tenderly took my mustard seed of faith. So, in faith, I began to fight.

I looked to His Word, and it assured me over and over. Luke 1:37 (AMP) says, "With God nothing [is or ever] shall be impossible." Jeremiah 32:17 (NLT) declares, "O Sovereign Lord! You made the heavens and the earth by your strong hand and powerful arm. Nothing is too hard for you!" In Genesis 18:14 (NLT), we read, "Is anything too hard for the Lord?"

Since then, there have been moments when the tentacles of fright mastered me. Times I felt overcome with worry about one of my sons or our finances. Incidents that triggered memories of past marital pain. And I surrendered *yet again.* But more so, I've experienced days when the mountain moved ever so slightly and my mustard-seed faith grew. When I was overcome by God's peace amid struggles with my kids, marriage, or money. When my fear-fighting faith made strides. I celebrate each step as I march on in battle surrounded by a mighty God, held by His powerful hand.

In the end, our Savior will stand, along with you and me, holding the victory trophy high. No more fear. No more worry. Until then, let's move those Alps.

> If you have faith the size of the smallest seed,
> nothing will be impossible for you.[30]

Reflection

1. What mountain do you currently face? Tell the Lord about it.

2. Open your hands to Him and offer your mustard seed of faith.

Prayer

Dear Savior,

As I hold out my mustard seed of faith, I claim this promise: "Nothing will be impossible for You!" Thank You, Jesus, that my smallest beginning of belief can move the biggest of mountains in my life. I trust You today with *everything*.

Amen

---

[30] Priscilla Shirer and Gina Detwiler, *The Prince Warriors and the Unseen Invasion* (Nashville, TN: B&H Kids, 2021).

#26

Relief in Release

Peter came to Jesus and asked,
"Lord, how many times shall I forgive my brother
or sister who sins against me? Up to seven times?"
Jesus answered, "I tell you, not seven times,
but seventy-seven times."
Matthew 18:21–22

The text message said, "Forgiven people forgive."

"What?" I yelled as my blood pressure rose. I threw my phone on the bed. How *dare* she send that to me on this miserable morning! How *dare* she insinuate that I should pardon the person who heaped wrong upon wrong on me! The hurt was too deep, the offenses too many.

My heart still skips when I remember that text years ago. When this memory floods in, I often recall today's Scripture in Matthew. Peter's question is sandwiched between Jesus's speech regarding discipline in the church and the parable of the unforgiving servant. I am curious about Peter's question. Was he trying to appear generous in extending his own mercy limit to seven times when the rabbis preached that the magic mercy number was three? Or was Peter a victim of multiple wrongdoings? Did he want to know how much clemency is too much?

Christ's response was above and beyond Peter's and the rabbis' numbers. His heart for His followers is that we forgive not three times, not seven times, but *seventy times seven.* His point was not that we forgive our offenders 490 times but an infinite number if necessary.

I don't know who your person is or the anguish they caused. It could be they have never asked for forgiveness, and maybe they never will. Possibly they continue to hurt you, or perhaps they are no longer living. These are difficult waters to navigate.

When we refuse to forgive, we heap inner torment upon ourselves. We turn the key to our personal prison door and secure the lock tighter and tighter each day. Bitterness brews and churns like acid in our core. Jesus understood that holding on to a grudge will cause us (not the one who hurt us) ongoing misery.

Ah, but there is relief in release.

Friend, it is Resurrection season, the season of the ultimate triumph of overcoming. A time when we focus on the cross, where Christ took on and took away our sins. Forever. Psalm 103:12 tells us, "As far as the east is from the west, so far has he removed our transgressions from us." I believe the only reason we are capable of this type of release is because of the cross and the incalculable grace, mercy, and pardon we've been given. And since God's Spirit lives in us, He gives us the strength to let go.

It is important to note that none of this means you allow a harmful, hurtful person to stay in your life. There is a difference between forgiveness and wisdom for safety. Sometimes it is vital to get help from a pastor, counselor, or trusted friend to navigate these lanes. It is a journey, and it is messy.

The sender of that text was right. Forgiven people do forgive. According to Jesus, this is God's best for us. My journey in this area has been ugly and oh so painful. Yet, by God's grace, I have forgiven and forgiven again (what feels like 490 times) those who have wronged me. I have felt the sweet relief of release and the magnificent gratitude to God for the mercy of the cross.

> If I say, "Yes, I forgive, but I cannot forget," as though the God who twice a day washes all the sands on all the shores of all the world could not wash such memories from my mind, then I know nothing of Calvary love.[31]

Reflection

1. Read the parable of the unforgiving servant in Matthew 18:21–35. Do you see yourself in this story? Record your thoughts.

2. Read Ephesians 4:32 as you think of the person (or people) who've wronged you and hurt you. Consider the steps you will take this very day toward forgiveness.

Prayer

Dear Savior,

Words cannot adequately express my gratitude to You. You have removed my sins as far as the east is from the west! May I find Your strength and relief in release. Help me navigate these tough waters, because I cannot do this without You.

Amen

---

[31] Amy Carmichael, "If—Part 2 (Calvary Love)," *Women of Christianity*, May 4, 2011, https://womenofchristianity.com/if-part-2-calvary-love-by-amy-carmichael.

Days 27-33
Judea and Perea

My Hope Is Built on Nothing Less
(Verses 1, 2, and Refrain)

My hope is built on nothing less
than Jesus' blood and righteousness;
I dare not trust the sweetest frame,
but wholly lean on Jesus' name.

When darkness veils his lovely face,
I rest on his unchanging grace;
in every high and stormy gale,
my anchor holds within the veil.

On Christ, the solid Rock, I stand:
all other ground is sinking sand;
all other ground is sinking sand.[32]

---

[32] Edward Mote, "My Hope Is Built on Nothing Less," 1834.

#27

The Light of Life

I am the light of the world. If you follow me,
you won't have to walk in darkness,
because you will have the light that leads to life.
John 8:12 (NLT)

Gloomy clouds dawned in the morning sky once again. The dreariness outside and the relentless bad news on my TV screen merged with palpable fear and underlying depression. It all felt suffocating.

From the edge of my bed, I gazed out my window and prayed. As I asked Christ to lift the dismal, heavy weight off my chest and bolster me for another long day, a stunning beam of sunlight broke through the clouds. A fitting symbol of truth I had failed to remember: Jesus is the Light of the World and the light of my life.

In that morning moment, God shone a brilliant dose of bravery into my troubled soul. As a result, a shift took place in my spirit as I began to focus more on Christ's light and less on the shadows of the world. I turned to key promises in Scripture to boost my courage, and I sought out feel-good stories on social media. With great intention, I reduced my intake of the sad, negative news I had spent too much time consuming and increased my intake of God's Word, the *true* Good News. I put key Scriptures on my phone and stuck them on sticky notes near my bed and computer as reminders.

Unfortunately, days still come when I fail to remember, and the shadows press in *yet again.* Can you relate? So, once again, I open my Bible to those trusted, hope-filled verses. Words that prompt me to shift my gaze to the brightness of Christ, the one who called Himself the Light of the World.

Join me! Let's bravely fix our thoughts on the Light of Life as we dive into the following verses to boost our courage:

- *Christ is the light that leads to life.* "I am the light of the world. If you follow me, you won't have to walk in darkness, because you will have the light that leads to life." (John 8:12)
- *The Lamb is our light.* "The city has no need of sun or moon, for the glory of God illuminates the city, and the Lamb is its light." (Revelation 21:23 NLT)
- *The Lord is our forever light.* "Your sun will never set; your moon will not go down. For the Lord will be your everlasting light. Your days of mourning will come to an end." (Isaiah 60:20 NLT)
- *We need not fear because of His light.* "The Lord is my light and my salvation—so why should I be afraid?" (Psalm 27:1 NLT)

Even on our gloomiest days, may the darkness remind us to turn to these truths and allow them to permeate our spirits with boldness as we bask in the stunning beam of good news: Christ is the Light of Life.

Help me to understand that, because I'm Yours, light is shining in my darkness whether I can behold it or understand it.[33]

Reflection

1. For more insights, read John 1:4–5, Isaiah 9:2, and 2 Corinthians 4:6.

2. Consider the effect that negative media stories have on you. What brave steps might you take to decrease your intake of gloomy news and increase the brightness of Christ?

Prayer

Dear Savior,

You are the light of the world, and I ask You *yet again* to be the light of my life. I choose to focus on Your good truths instead of the negativity in the world. Bolster me with Your light and courage on this day.

Amen

---

[33] Beth Moore, *Praying God's Word: Breaking Free from Spiritual Strongholds* (Nashville, TN: B&H Publishing Group, 2009).

#28

When You Pray

He said to them, "When you pray, say:
'Father, hallowed be your name, your kingdom come.
Give us each day our daily bread. Forgive us our sins,
for we also forgive everyone who sins against us.
And lead us not into temptation.'"
Luke 11:2–4

When I was ten, my mom encouraged me to memorize the entire Lord's Prayer. She gave me a typed-out copy from Matthew 6 to carry around as I worked on it. All through my life, I have been grateful these words of Christ live in my mind. They have brought me comfort, inspiration, and connection with God.

Prayer was a priority in the life of Christ. Luke 5:16 says, "Jesus often withdrew to lonely places and prayed." The Savior not only prayed in times of quiet but also during significant life events: His baptism, when He fed the crowds, His transfiguration, the night before He chose the Twelve, at the tomb of Lazarus, in the garden of Gethsemane, and on the cross.

There are two places in the Gospels where we discover the words of what is commonly known as the Lord's Prayer. The entire portion is found early in the Messiah's ministry in the Sermon on the Mount (Matthew 6:9–15). A shortened version appears in

Luke, toward the end of Jesus's time on earth. And here, after a disciple asked Him to teach them to pray as John had taught his followers. This is the only recorded time one of the disciples asked Jesus to teach them anything.

I have often used these words as a pattern for prayer, taking each section in pieces. This is what I'd like us to do with the key passage from Luke 11 on this twenty-eighth day of our Easter journey together. I encourage you to look up the corresponding Scriptures as you pray aloud to your heavenly Father.

Father, hallowed be Your name. Honor His name, starting with praise. Praise was a mainstay in Christ's prayers, so let's do likewise and give God praise before we launch into our requests. (See Psalm 145:3.)

Your kingdom come. Our hope is not in the world but in God's kingdom. Pray for opportunities to usher in His kingdom today by being His light to those around us. (See Matthew 12:50.)

Give us each day our daily bread. One of God's names is Jehovah Jireh, which means "God is Provider." Pray for God to provide for your needs and the needs of others. (See Proverbs 30:8.)

Forgive us our sins. Let us sit before the Lord and confess our sins to Him. Then thank Him for His unconditional forgiveness. (See 1 John 1:8–9.)

Forgive everyone who sins against us. Remembering how He has forgiven us, let us take time to think about those we are holding grudges against. Those we need to forgive. Ask Him for the strength and courage to do so. (See Colossians 3:13.)

Lead us not into temptation. We need to ask for God's strength to overcome whatever we are struggling with and to flee temptation. (See 2 Thessalonians 3:3.)

It is remarkable to think that even to this day, Jesus, the High Priest, continues to pray for us from His glorious place in heaven, seated at the right hand of God. The Bible tells us that the Son of God makes perpetual intercession for those who belong to Him.

This overwhelms my mind, yet it brings me immense hope and a feeling of deep love and gratitude to my Savior.

> First, *Thy* name, *Thy* kingdom, *Thy* will;
> then, give *us*, forgive *us*, lead *us*, deliver *us*.
> The lesson is of more importance than we think.
> In true worship the Father must be first, must be all.[34]

Reflection

1. Have you committed the Lord's Prayer to memory? If not, I encourage you to do so.

2. Read Romans 8:35, Hebrews 7:25, and 1 John 2:1. Close your eyes as you picture the Messiah interceding for you at the Father's right hand.

Prayer

Dear Savior,

I picture You now, at this very moment, interceding for me at the Father's right hand. With all that is within me, I thank You. I am filled with hope and profound gratitude today for this practical pattern for prayer.

Amen

---

[34] Andrew Murray, *Lord, Teach Us to Pray* (Conshohocken, PA: Infinity, 2015), 26.

#29
Behold!

Behold, we are going up to Jerusalem, and the Son of Man
will be betrayed to the chief priests and to the scribes;
and they will condemn Him to death, and deliver Him
to the Gentiles to mock and to scourge and to crucify.
And the third day He will rise again.
Matthew 20:18–19 (NKJV)

The solemn rabbi strode ahead of His disciples as a red-hot sun
beat down on their gravel trail.

The final trek.

In their last journey to Jerusalem, Jesus spoke of upcoming
events in traditional rabbinic custom: students follow the teacher.
But then He changed His approach. He stopped and pulled His
beloved Twelve close, apart from the crowd of followers. His
words, of utmost importance, required intimacy with undistracted
disciples.

Here their instructor (for the third and final time) provided a
verbal blueprint of what was to come. A map of the terrible trials
soon to unfold. His heart desired to prepare His students for the
sorrow and suffering they would witness.

He addressed them with an intensity meant to prick their attention by beginning with "Behold." This word is translated in the Greek as *idou*, meaning "Behold! See! Lo! Look!"[35]

This same pronouncement was made by the angel who spoke to Joseph in a dream about Mary's baby, the anointed Son of God (Matthew 1:23). The Father uttered it when His only begotten Son emerged from the water after His baptism (Matthew 3:17).

It is a term that holds weight and implores listeners to open their ears. Even still, the men did not understand what Christ meant, or perhaps they were not ready to hear it. Or bear it.

They did not want to face the shadow of the cross that fell on the road to Jerusalem that day.

The process of transformation can take oh so long, even for the ones who personally walked behind and beside the Master. But we know the end of the story. We know that eleven of the pupils passed their class with the highest of eternal marks.

He is patient with the process.

As modern disciples, while we continue our transformation with the Savior this Lenten season, let us *Behold! Lo! See! Look!* As we get closer to the closing chapters of Christ's earthly story, the shadow of the cross looms large. May we open our hearts and allow our Teacher to inject His life and thoughts into our very souls.

> The real son of God is at your side. He is beginning to turn you into the same kind of thing as Himself. He is beginning, so to speak, to "inject" His kind of life and thought ... into you; beginning to turn the tin soldier into a live man. The part of you that does not like it is the part that is still tin.[36]

---

[35] James Strong, *The New Strong's Exhaustive Concordance of the Bible* (Nashville, TN: Thomas Nelson, 1995).

[36] C. S. Lewis, *Mere Christianity* (San Francisco, CA: HarperOne, 2015).

Reflection

1. Read additional *idou* Scriptures in the King James
    Version of Matthew 2:1, Matthew 2:13, and Matthew
    26:45.

2. Have you invited the Teacher to walk alongside you,
    to *inject* His life and thoughts into you? Record your
    contemplations.

Prayer

Dear Savior,

I behold You! Thank You for beginning a transformative work
in me. I invite You to infuse Yourself into my very soul. I choose to
follow behind You, my patient Teacher, as I step in the shadow of
the cross.

Amen

#30

Mrs. Zebedee

You do not know what you ask. Are you able to drink
the cup that I am about to drink, and be baptized
with the baptism that I am baptized with?
Matthew 20:22 (NKJV)

I know women like Salome Zebedee. They frequent Little League fields, swim lessons, schools, and karate classes. These overly proud and aggressive moms want their kids to be the goalies for the soccer team or the leads in the play. You might know a few of these gals too.

The mother of James and John, the sons of Zebedee, came to
Jesus with her sons. She knelt respectfully to ask a favor.
Matthew 20:20 (NLT)

After Jesus asked her what she wanted, she requested that He let her sons sit in places of honor in His kingdom: one on His right side and one on His left.

A bold, ambitious request. As a mom of boys, I am captivated by this passage, giggling as I read. One of the first things I notice is that Mama did the asking, not her grown-up sons. Her "boys" lurked behind her while the rest of the incredulous disciples listened in. The Son of God had called these two "Sons of Thunder," yet they sure did not live up to that name on this day.

Mrs. Zebedee was devoted to the Savior. She had left her husband to join her children and follow Jesus. She went on to witness His crucifixion, and she was one of the women to arrive at the empty tomb after His resurrection. A member of the faithful. But still ... a mother.

And how about the timing of this request? It came immediately after Christ predicted His death. James and John stood next to Him as He described the horrors of what was to come. It seems they listened but did not hear, imagining a powerful kind of kingdom with the Messiah as monarch. The Zebedee trio had their eyes on thrones of glory, not on cups of agony, filtering out what they did not want to hear.

Jesus asked if James and John could suffer what He was to suffer, and they rapidly answered, "We can" (verse 21).

And they did.

If Mama had known, she never would have asked. James was the first of the disciples to die, beheaded by King Herod. John, called "the one whom Jesus loved," lived into old age, his life story filled with persecution, torture, and exile.

I see myself in the Zebedees. Often I have selective hearing or selective seeing as I gloss over the tough truths of Scripture, my focus poles apart from God's. I sift out the sour and replace it with sweet. Certain verses are easier to digest than those centered on instructions, the cost of faith, suffering, and the persecution of the church.

Salome Zebedee eventually saw the realities of the kingdom, because her family drank from the bitter and most beautiful cup of Christ. Her eyes and ears awakened to a new kind of King.

Jesus told them, "You will indeed drink from my bitter cup."
Matthew 10:23 (NLT)

Reflection

1. Search your heart. Do you notice yourself filtering out certain Scriptures? Why do you do that?

2. What do you want to do the next time that happens? Record your thoughts.

Prayer

Dear Savior,

Please open the eyes of my heart to see, hear, and know what You have for me in the entirety of Your Word. The bitter and the sweet. The suffering and the glory.

Amen

#31

What Do You Want Me to Do for You?

"What do you want me to do for you?" Jesus asked him.
The blind man said, "Rabbi, I want to see."
Mark 10:51

As we stand on the threshold of Holy Week, I'd like us to consider the question Jesus asked blind Bartimaeus in Mark 10: "What do you want Me to do for you?" First, however, I would like to personalize it by asking myself, *What do I want God to do for me?*

I realize it may feel selfish to ask this question. God is not a genie; we can't just present a list before Him and ask Him for stuff.

Or can we?

Jesus traveled with a caravan on the traditional route from Galilee to Jerusalem. Jerusalem, the sacred city, where the Son of God would enter triumphantly on a donkey and leave carrying a cross.

Jericho was the last stop before the caravan would make the strenuous climb to Jerusalem. This route was most likely crowded with beggars during the Passover season, and here is where Jesus met Bartimaeus. When the blind man heard the crowd passing and the murmur that Jesus of Nazareth was in their midst, he repeatedly shouted to Christ using the Messianic title "Son of David." To call Jesus this name indicates that the blind man believed Christ to be the Messiah and Healer.

So Bartimaeus gave it his all.

In Mark 10:47, "shout" translates from the Greek word *krazo*.[37] This means "to cry out noisily with an urgent scream or shriek." Even though others tried to quiet him, the blind man made himself impossible to ignore, and the Son of David stopped and told the disciples to call Bartimaeus to Him. Then came the question. (Don't you love the questions Christ asked?) Such humility and vulnerability are required in the answer. After the blind man replied, Christ healed Him and went on to say, "Your faith has healed you."

Now, back to you and me. What do we want God to do? Is it time to give it our all? To cry out as Bartimaeus did? This idea struck me some years ago during a severe trial. I prayed for everyone else involved in the heartache, even those barely afflicted, daily. Yet I did not pray much for myself. I knew others were lifting my situation to the Lord and took deep comfort from that. But I was the one intimately acquainted with my legion of needs. So why didn't I pray for myself?

In taking an honest look, I saw fear and guilt in my answer. I was afraid God would not answer my requests in the way I would like—or not at all. There was also a prick of guilt in focusing too much on myself. I thought of the millions of others who suffered much worse than I did.

However, I remembered that God's Word says it is okay— and more so, welcomed. I found sixty-seven "asking" verses in the Bible. Even Christ begged the Father to do something for

---

[37] James Strong, *The New Strong's Exhaustive Concordance of the Bible* (Nashville, TN: Thomas Nelson, 1995), 2896.

Him (Matthew 26:39). We see numerous examples of individuals pouring out their hearts, humbly and vulnerably, in petition to God. Scripture beckons us to make requests of our Father.

He asks us to ask. Again and again.

So let's give it our all—as Bartimaeus did!

> The greatest tragedy in life is the prayers
> that go unanswered because they go unasked.[38]

Reflection

1. Read the following "asking" verses: Psalm 5:3, Matthew 21:22, Luke 11:9, and John 14:13–14.

2. What do you want God to do for you? Write your answer as a prayer.

Prayer

Dear Savior,

It amazes me that I can ask You for what I want, that I can invite You to intervene in my life. Teach me to request humbly and vulnerably without guilt or fear. Help me to trust You with my requests.

Amen

---

[38] Mark Batterson, *The Circle Maker: Praying Circles Around Your Biggest Dreams and Greatest Fears* (Grand Rapids, MI: Zondervan, 2016).

#32

It's So Nice to Be Seen!

"I tell you the truth," Jesus said,
"this poor widow has given more than all the rest
of them. For they have given a tiny part of their surplus,
but she, poor as she is, has given everything she has."
Luke 21:3–4 (NLT)

As the haggard-looking woman walked through the door of the church, I handed her a meal ticket and said, "It's so nice to see you." She muttered a reply I didn't catch. So I asked her to repeat herself, leaned in closer, and clearly heard, "It's so nice to be seen."

At first glance, she appeared to be in her fifties, but on closer inspection I realized she was much younger. Her face told the story of a life roughly lived. She wore a slightly torn gray sweater and baggy jeans, and she accepted her ticket with holey gloves.

I was in downtown San Diego with my family, serving an early Christmas meal to the homeless. My job was to hand out meal tickets and track the number of people coming in on a wall chart. As I worked and greeted, my eyes kept floating to where this woman sat.

After the meal, there was music and prayer and an opportunity to donate. The service organization leader challenged the people who lived on the street to give out of their lack to a little boy in

Africa. The man held up a picture of the boy and told his sad story. My gaze was discreetly riveted on my friend in gray. As the leader spoke, she shoved her hand into her pocket, and when the basket made its way to her, she dropped in cash. A bright smile beamed on her weathered face while tears soaked my riveted eyes.

This memory stirs my heart and pulls my mind to the story of a woman in the gospel of Luke.

Luke writes of a day when the Messiah sat at the temple treasury in the court of women and watched the people coming in. He saw the rich make a big show as they dropped their gifts in the ornate collection box. Then He observed a poor widow (a triple curse: poor, widowed, and a woman) drop two small coins into the box. The Message version says, "She gave extravagantly what she couldn't afford." I wonder if she heard Christ as He praised her aloud to the disciples. Did she notice that He saw her? Luke makes no mention of this.

I imagine if the poor widow heard His words of admiration and understood that He saw her, she may have felt like the lady I met that December day: grateful to be seen, and beyond this, gratified to know that her sacrifice counted for the kingdom. We read about this woman in Scripture to this day because Jesus saw her model genuine devotion to God and His purposes. She mattered.

I believe Jesus beams with joy when the people He sees see others. When He watches us pour our time and treasures on humans whom He adores. When we care for His children and express irrepressible generosity to His kingdom causes.

To know we've been sighted by our Savior is a prize in itself. Then there's a calling. A calling to faithfully notice those whom the Lord places in our path. To begin each morning by asking Him to show us who needs to know today that they matter to God—that they matter to us.

It really is so nice to be seen.

El Roi means "The God who sees me."
Ro'iy in the original Hebrew can be translated as *shepherd*,
or as *seeing, looking,* or *gazing.* In other words, when we feel
most invisible and forgotten by everyone else,
we can remember that God does see us.[39]

Reflection

1. What does it mean to know God sees you and treasures you, whether you are doing kingdom work or not?

2. Read the following expressions of faith: Matthew 8:10, Matthew 25:40, and James 1:27.

Prayer

Dear Savior,

I am eternally grateful that You see me. Thank You for placing the story of this generous widow in the Bible as a reminder of what You consider valuable. Keep me faithful to see the unseen and to do the kingdom work that brings You joy.

Amen

---

39 Hope Bolinger, "Meaning and Importance of God's Name 'El Roi'—The God Who Sees Me," Bible Study Tools, https://www.Biblestudytools.com/bible-study/topical-studies/reasons-to-praise-god-as-el-roi.html.

#33

Extravagant

Truly I tell you, wherever this gospel is preached
throughout the world, what she has done
will also be told, in memory of her.
Matthew 26:13

The part was called "The Girl" and my eleven-year-old self wanted it desperately. The youth department at my church had announced upcoming tryouts for its spring musical. Determined to get the role, I practiced and prayed and prayed and practiced. The Girl was a main character with not one but *two* solos.

When the choir director read my name at the first rehearsal, I screamed with joy. I got the part! When I arrived home that evening, I raced inside to begin my research. Each person in the show was to read Scripture passages about the Bible character their role was based on. The main characters were Christ's closest friends but written as kids. The Girl was designed with Mary, the sister of Lazarus and Martha, in mind.

Unfortunately, there are no pictures from that night, but I remember it well. I wore a white dress and sandals. My mom painstakingly styled my hair in what we called the "half up half down" do. She applied lipstick and blush to my stage face. My family sat in the front row of the big church sanctuary; the proud smiles of my grandparents lit up the room.

I loved every minute of the performance. That is, until my second solo. The Girl slowly poured a jar of expensive perfume on the head of Christ in preparation for His burial. (I mostly pretended, as there was *no way* I would have touched the head of the boy who played Jesus.) As the stage lights shone on me, I got lost in my character. I imagined the deep love Mary felt for her friend, that she would honor Him in this elaborate, intimate way. Tears trickled down my cheeks as I fought to keep my voice from cracking. It wasn't pretty, but I kept it together and finished the song.

Like with the night of my spring musical, there are no photographs of Mary as she stood next to the Savior holding an alabaster jar full of pricey perfume. Yet I can picture the scene.

Jesus and His disciples reclined at a table after a satisfying meal. His days with them were coming to a rapid end, but His men still did not comprehend this truth. However, Mary knew Christ's death was imminent, and in this powerful moment she chose to anoint the one who loved her first. But the men gathered around were offended by her deed. The Message says, "When the disciples saw what was happening, they were furious. 'That's criminal! This could have been sold for a lot and the money handed out to the poor'" (Matthew 26:8).

The Messiah rebuked the disciples for their response and called Mary's act of worship "beautiful" (verse 10). My favorite part is that He went on to say that her alabaster sacrifice would always be remembered. Always.

As I gaze into this story of Jesus and Mary, tears run down my face once again. I am awed by this bold, vulnerable, and extravagant gift; I am moved by this extravagant love. After all these years, this still gets me.

"In pouring this fragrant oil on My body,
she did it for My burial."
Matthew 26:12 (NKJV)

Reflection

1. Read Matthew 26:11. What do you think Jesus's statement regarding the poor means?

2. With Mary's example as inspiration, record in your journal how you will extravagantly adore your Savior this Easter season.

Prayer

Dear Savior,

Mary loved You because You loved her first. May this picture of her extravagant example inspire me to adore You as she did. Today, I choose to return Your love with my "alabaster jar," the gift of my life.

Amen

Days 34-40
Holy Week

The Old Rugged Cross
(Verse 4 and Refrain)

To that old rugged cross I will ever be true,
its shame and reproach gladly bear;
then he'll call me some day to my home far away,
where his glory forever I'll share.

So I'll cherish the old rugged cross,
till my trophies at last I lay down;
I will cling to the old rugged cross,
and exchange it some day for a crown.[40]

---

[40] George Bennard, The Old Rugged Cross, 1913.

#34
The Temple Cleanse

He said to them, "The Scriptures declare,
'My Temple will be called a house of prayer,'
but you have turned it into a den of thieves!"
Matthew 21:13 (NLT)

With the dawn of a new year, Israel's holy calendar ushered in the Passover and the Feast of Unleavened Bread. Expectation wafted through the Jerusalem air as Holy Week began. A week that consecutively occurred with an unseen, divine timetable. Here in Jerusalem, both converged, as the magnitude of time on earth was forever altered to Before Christ and After Death: Anno Domini.

Sunday: Prophecy was fulfilled. "Rejoice, O people of Zion! Shout in triumph, O people of Jerusalem! Look, your king is coming to you. He is righteous and victorious, yet he is humble, riding on a donkey—riding on a donkey's colt." (Zechariah 9:9 NLT)

The radical rabbi rode triumphantly into the streets of Jerusalem for Passover. He straddled a donkey as crowds shouted, "Hosanna!" (meaning "Save us!") and placed palm branches down in worship before Him as the long-awaited Messiah-King.

Monday morning: "Jesus entered the Temple and began to drive out all the people buying and selling animals for sacrifice. He knocked over the tables of the money changers and the chairs of those selling doves" (Matthew 21:12 NLT).

The Passover was the year's highlight for the Jews, who traveled to Jerusalem from different regions and countries to commemorate it. Each family was required to meet two conditions to participate. The first was an animal sacrifice (usually a dove), available in the temple marketplace at exorbitant prices. The next was a temple tax, due upon arrival. Because many of the multitudes were foreign, they had to exchange their currency for that of the Romans (Jerusalem was a Roman-occupied territory), and corrupt traders abounded to "help" the travelers do so, for a steep price.

The crooks turned God's house of prayer into a den of thieves.

As the Son of God entered the busy house of the Lord that Monday morning and took in the scene before Him, He erupted in outrage. His voice carried above the crowd and echoed against the white marble walls. Acting with a king's authority, He picked up a whip made from cords and drove out the offenders. His heart was heavy, burdened for the scammed worshippers and a broken sacrificial system.

From a subdued Savior, humble on a donkey, to the righteous, enraged Son in His Father's house, Christ established His position as King. The Bible stories that get the most play are the ones of gentle Jesus: with the children, feeding crowds, healing the sick. Yet sometimes, to encounter Him anew, we must center in on His incensed zeal toward outlaws and hypocrites. His hatred toward injustice. His passion for the oppressed.

He is not a one-dimensional king.

As we read the Messiah's words each day of Passion Week, let us experience Him in fresh ways, in all His dimensions.

Blessed is He who comes in the name of the Lord!
Blessed is the coming kingdom of our father David!
Hosanna in the highest heaven!
Mark 11:9–10

Reflection

1. Which aspect of Jesus's character do you tend to overemphasize in your mind? The humble King on a donkey or a righteous, incensed Son of God? Why?

2. With upturned hands and eyes closed, thank Him for all of His dimensions.

Prayer

Dear Savior,

Hosanna in the highest! Blessed is He who comes in the name of the Lord! Come save us, King Jesus. As I hear Your words during these Holy days, may I encounter You anew.

Amen

#35

The Whole Law
and the Prophets

The most important commandment is this: ...
"Love the Lord your God with all your heart,
all your soul, all your mind, and all your strength."
The second is equally important: "Love your neighbor as
yourself." No other commandment is greater than these.
Mark 12:30–31 (NLT)

Later in the day, after the purge of the temple, we find Jesus again moving about the beautiful temple court with its massive columns, staircases, and lampstands, dressed in a simple brown tunic made from cotton. The Savior is at the end of His public ministry, in His last conflict with the Jewish authorities.

Christ spent a great deal of time during His final week in this place. As He taught His followers, He also interacted with the religious authorities. They wore ostentatious priestly garments made of purple linen decorated with gold, blue, and scarlet yarn. Their long tassels dragged—a sign meant to prove they were serious scholars of the covenant—as they marched the temple courts preparing to accost the man from Galilee. These rabbis wanted to get rid of Him, yet they were afraid of the crowds (Luke 22:2). Tensions toward Him were building to the boiling point due to His constant criticisms of their hypocrisy and His outburst in the temple.

They'd had enough of Jesus.

The plan was to ask a series of questions designed to trick Him. As they debated with Christ, a teacher of the law asked, "Of all the commandments, which is the most important?" (Mark 12:28 NLT). At this point, it was high-fives all around because this Pharisee had asked the question that would finally stump the Galilean. But the celebration stopped when Jesus answered, and the answer went beyond the question.

His words fell like grenades.

Christ summed up the significance of the entire rule of God with all its moral obligations by equalizing these two commands: love God first and then love others as you love yourself. A startling statement. These men had devoted their lives to collating more than six hundred laws. They scrutinized the order of their importance and placed them as heavy weights on the Jews. How dare Jesus sum all that up to grace and truth.

But He did not stop there. Matthew 22:40 (NASB) tells us Jesus went on to say, "Upon these two commandments hang the whole Law and the Prophets." The whole of it? Pause here with me as we take in the magnitude of this statement, because everything in God's Word depends on it. Let His words hang in the air, just as they did that day two thousand years ago. I love the way Eugene Patterson puts it in The Message: "These two commands are pegs; everything in God's Law and the Prophets hangs from them."

Days before He hung on a cross to His death, the Savior flipped the script when He emphasized relationships over rules. Love over law.

After that, no one dared to ask him any more questions.
Mark 12:34 (NLT)

Reflection

1. Why did no one dare ask Jesus any more questions?

2. Read Leviticus 19:18, Deuteronomy 6:5, and John 1:17. Let these words hang in the air.

Prayer

Dear Savior,

You altered the entirety of the religious system when You established love over law and relationships over rules. I thank You that I do not have to try to keep six hundred rules to earn Your favor. Your grace is the peg I hang my life on.

Amen

#36

A New Command

Now I am giving you a new commandment: Love each
other. Just as I have loved you, you should love each
other. Your love for one another will prove to the world
that you are my disciples.
John 13:34–35 (NLT)

After the final dinner.

After a foot-washing by a King who came to serve.

After this band of men watched their traitorous companion
leave the table.

The air spun with tangled emotion as their leader's words
filled the space. This was no suggestion in the last teaching before
Jesus's death. In this lesson, we discover an if-then principle: "If
you love the way I have loved, then people will know you are My
disciples." And part two goes like this: If we represent our Savior
well, then others will find Him winsome.

Jesus often spoke about "doing" love. We have covered much
of this "doing," this passion of Christ, in these pages, haven't we?
Because of the somberness of this week and the ultimate act of
love our Savior is about to express, I believe today is the perfect
place in this love story to recap the love list.

Our Savior:

- Healed the sick (Matthew 14:14)
- Raised the dead (John 11:38–44)
- Cast out demons (Matthew 8:16)
- Fed the hungry (Matthew 15:32)
- Cherished children (Mark 10:13–16)
- Hung out with sinners and the despised (Mark 2:15)
- Preached the kingdom of God (Mark 6:34)
- Prayed for His believers (John 17:20–21)
- Forgave sins (Matthew 26:28)

Love in action.

And this new command translates to His followers today.

Never have I witnessed a demon cast or the dead raised. But in the ever-increasing decades of my church life, I've observed communities and individuals who acted out Christ's example, accounts that could fill volumes. My eyes tear up as I recall groups gathered at death's bedside. I remember the walks in the streets to share food with, befriend, and provide medical care for the homeless, drug addicted, and prostitutes. The college group who bathed kids in buckets in Mexico while picking lice out of their hair. I've heard the truth of Christ preached and I've attended prayer gatherings where precious souls pled in petition to God for their fellow church members and the world outside the sanctuary doors. And I have known individuals who forgave the unforgivable, even the despised. Mountains of passion in action, beautiful examples of the Savior's command to His disciples at the Last Supper.

The church can be embarrassingly imperfect. Yet when Christ-followers carry out His greatest command and "do" love in action, they are a radiant representation of their Savior.

The kind of love that God created and demonstrated
is a costly one because it involves sacrifice and presence.
It's a love that operates more like a sign language
than being spoken outright.[41]

Reflection

1. Think of a few people you know who have exemplified
   the Savior beautifully. Record your thoughts on how you
   might follow their examples.

2. How will you "do" love well today?

Prayer

Dear Savior,

I consider with soberness that Your greatest commandment
was not merely a suggestion but a command. Because of this, I
commit myself to representing You well. May others know of You
because of my deeds of love.

Amen

---

[41] Bob Goff, *Love Does: Discover a Secretly Incredible Life in an Ordinary World* (Nashville, TN: Thomas Nelson, 2012).

#37

I Am the Vine

I am the vine; you are the branches.
Whoever abides in me and I in him,
he it is that bears much fruit, for apart from me
you can do nothing. ... By this my Father is glorified,
that you bear much fruit and so prove to be my disciples.
John 15:5, 8 (ESV)

On the threshold of zero hour, before a trek to a garden, our Savior delivered His very last "I AM" statement: "I am the vine." Jesus made a total of seven "I AM" declarations, and this final one He saved for the intimacy of the upper room as His beloved Eleven enfolded Him.

As I read this passage in John, I have no struggle with the vine-and-branch metaphor. I find myself quite at home here. You see, vines are a big deal in my town. We are a mecca for wine enthusiasts with miles and miles of rolling hills covered with the grapevines of more than fifty wineries.

I am also quite at home with Christ's assertion that to bear fruit for God, I (the branch) need to hang on to Him (the vine). In my case, it's more of a white-knuckled grip, because when I let go, it ain't pretty. But that's just it. I cling so tightly because I've learned that the secret of the Christian life is in the abiding. To remain in Jesus means to hold strong to the precious, powerful vine.

Jesus implored the disciples to make their home in Him. To abide in Him. We understand how vital this missive is when we realize that He used the words *abide* and *abides* ten times in seven verses.

Dear twenty-first-century disciple, have you made your home in Him? The Bible tells us if we believe in Jesus Christ, we are "in" Him and are attached to Him. No matter where we are in our Christ-journey, we can experience this connection more deeply when we read the Bible, pray, and commit His Word to memory, as we spend time in reflection, grafting His truth into our souls.

As we do so, we produce a bounty and shine for the Savior as His disciples. Here's the fruit of the Spirit cluster as listed in Galatians 5:22–23 (ESV): love, joy, peace, patience, kindness, goodness, faithfulness, gentleness, and self-control.

Yet our objective isn't really the crop yield. Our sole goal (remember the secret of the Christian life?) is to live at home in Jesus, to simply *remain* in Him. The productivity of the fruit is the remarkable result of a life lived in the one who declared, "I am the vine."

John 15 depicts a kind of fruit-bearing that Christ prizes above all others. Every life that's attached to Him possesses the supernatural capacity to be stupendously productive.[42]

---

[42] Beth Moore, *Chasing Vines: Finding Your Way to an Immensely Fruitful Life* (Carol Stream, IL: Tyndale Momentum, 2020).

Reflection

1. Has your connection with Christ begun to direct your will, fill your mind, and transform you? If not, what can you do to change that?

2. If so, how does your (or rather, His) harvest display this attachment?

Prayer

Dear Savior,

My home is in You. I hold fast and tight to You, the true vine. I ask You to direct my will, fill my mind, and transform me. Lord, may I be Your ever-increasing, fruit-bearing, productive branch. A branch who gives You all the glory.

Amen

#38

Supreme Surrender

Then He went a little farther, fell to the ground,
and began to pray that if it were possible,
the hour might pass from Him. And He said,
"Abba, Father! All things are possible for You.
Take this cup away from Me. Nevertheless,
not what I will, but what You will."
Mark 14:35–36 (HCSB)

Have you endured acute anguish or severe trauma? So extreme
that it caused you to fall to the ground before the Lord?

Our Savior has.

Have you endured such deep distress in prayer that you sweat
teardrops of blood?

Our Savior has.

Have you ever prayed "The Prayer that Never Fails"?

Our Savior has.

Three times.

These events occurred in a garden called Gethsemane on the
night of Christ's betrayal and arrest. As the disciples dozed under
a dark sky, umbrellaed by cypress and olive trees, Jesus petitioned
and pleaded from the deepest recesses of His soul. He wrestled
with His Father.

The surrender story of the Messiah in the garden captivates me. You see, as God, He knew what lay ahead: supreme agony, separation from the Father, and more persecution and pain than any human could experience or would ever experience by bearing the sins of the entire world. The heavenly Father's plan lay solely on the shoulders of His Son. As Jesus grappled with submission, He begged His Father to allow Him a release. Yet ultimately, He submitted and prayed what author Jan Karon calls "The Prayer that Never Fails": Thy will be done.[43]

Because Christ chose surrender, the Father's will *was* done. I sit in awe of this supreme surrender as I revel in His love. The Son of God, our model of absolute submission, meets us when we fall to our knees in prayer. He holds our tears of anguish, and He patiently understands our struggle to yield. He is crazy about us. He gets us. We are His chosen and beloved.

Dear one, what is your surrender story? Is it time for you to lay down what needs laying down? Is it time to pray "The Prayer that Never Fails"? As you picture the Son of Man under the trees, tears of blood dropping to the dirt, pause in contemplation and allow this beautiful, heart-rending portrait speak to you.

> The battle is won. You may have thought it was won
> on Golgotha. It wasn't. You may have thought the sign
> of victory is the empty tomb. It isn't. The final battle was won
> in Gethsemane. And the sign of conquest is Jesus at peace
> in the olive trees. For it was in the Garden that He made

---

43   Alikay Wood, "Mitford Author Jan Karon Shares the 'Prayer That Never Fails,'" *Guideposts*, https://guideposts.org/positive-living/entertainment/books/mitford-author-jan-karon-shares-the-prayer-that-never-fails.

His decision that He would rather go to hell for you
than go to heaven without you.[44]

Reflection

1. Read Hebrews 5:7 and write it in your journal.

2. Claim the truth of this Scripture as you walk in your
   surrender story.

Prayer

Dear Savior,

How can it be? You chose me when You submitted Yourself
to Your Father in the garden. And because of that, in this holiest of
weeks, I revel in Your love and lay down what needs laying down.
Oh, how I thank You for the prayer that never fails.

Thy will be done.

Amen

---

[44] Max Lucado, *And the Angels Were Silent: The Final Week of Jesus* (Nashville, TN: Thomas Nelson, 2005).

#39

Words from the Cross

On the way, he took the Twelve aside
and said to them, "We are going up to Jerusalem,
and the Son of Man will be delivered over to the chief
priests and the teachers of the law. They will
condemn him to death and will hand him over
to the Gentiles to be mocked and flogged and crucified."
Matthew 20:17–19

No one in history deserved suffering less than our Savior. Yet He suffered the most. Christ Jesus was slapped, spit upon, stripped, scourged (beat with a whip with long leather tails and pieces of pottery, causing the body to go into shock), crucified, and abandoned by His Father. And so much more.

At nine o'clock on a blisteringly bright morning, outside the gates of Jerusalem, the Son of God staggered up a hill called Golgotha, which means "the place of the skull." By noon an eerie never-has-this-happened-before darkness covered the country. Three hours later, there was no more life in His body.

After driving nails into His limbs, ramming a crown of thorns into His head, then lifting Him on a cross, soldiers divided his garments and gambled for the pieces. The guards posted a sign of ridicule that read, "The King of the Jews." Two criminals hung with Him, one on His right and one on His left. Passersby mocked and taunted while others stood watching and weeping.

The tortured King, dying a thousand deaths, barely spoke. However, even in His torment, He uttered seven poignant statements from the cross. Join me this Easter weekend as we kneel before Him and listen to Him speak. With each account, I have included Scripture for further reading and contemplation.

"Father, forgive them, for they do not know what they are doing." (Luke 23:34)
See also Psalm 22:18 and Luke 6:27–28.

"I am thirsty." (John 19:28)
See also Psalm 22:15 and John 4:34.

"Today you will be with me in paradise." (Luke 23:43)
See also Luke 23:42 and Luke 19:10.

"Woman, here is your son." (John 19:26)
See also John 19:27 and John 16:32.

"*Eli, Eli, lema sabachthani?*" which means "My God, my God, why have you abandoned me?"
(Matthew 27:46 NLT)
See also Psalm 71:11 and Mark 15:33.

"It is finished [*Tetelestai*]." (John 19:30)
See also Matthew 27:50 and Luke 22:37.

"Father, I entrust my spirit into your hands!"
(Luke 23:46 NLT)
See also Psalm 31:5 and Mark 15:37.

At three o'clock, the darkness cleared. Jesus was dead. Our sin was forgiven by His unspeakable suffering—the highest price ever paid. These meaningful words uttered in His last hours display the constancy in His life's purpose and message: He came to die so that we might live!

When I Survey the Wondrous Cross

When I survey the wondrous Cross
On which the Prince of Glory died,
My richest gain, I count but loss
And pour contempt on all my pride.

See from His head, His hands, His feet,
Sorrow and love flow mingled down.
Did e'er such love and sorrow meet?
Or thorns compose so rich a crown?

Were the whole realm of nature mine,
That were a present far too small;
Love so amazing, so divine,
Demands my soul, my life, my all.[45]

Reflection

1. Out of the seven last statements of Jesus, which one troubles you the most? In your journal, record your thoughts.

---

[45] Isaac Watts, "When I Survey the Wondrous Cross," 1707.

2. Which statement inspires you the most? Record your words as praise to your Savior.

Prayer

Dear Savior,

I bow before You in awe and gratitude. Your words overcome me. So does Your love. On this Easter weekend, open my eyes anew to the cost of Your suffering and Your immeasurable love for me. Thank You for coming to die so that I might live!

Amen

#40

He Is Risen!

Woman, why are you crying?
Who is it you are looking for?
John 20:15

Peace be with you!
John 20:19

The Ones Who Stayed

Mary the mother of Jesus, Mary Magdalene, and several other women followed the Savior along the harrowing route to His death and witnessed the horrors of the crucifixion. Then, after the most traumatic of days, they gathered around the tomb where the soldiers had placed their Lord.

Why did this group trail their leader when others fled in terror? Sure, Mary stayed. Mothers usually do. But what about the others?

Perhaps their commitment to their King outweighed possible maltreatment. Maybe these loyal women had nowhere else to go but with their friend, this grieving mother, to her son's place of death. It could be they did not have the heart to walk away after what they had witnessed: the miraculous feedings, the healing touches, and the beauty of grace.

Three days later, Mary Magdalene and the other women carried aromatic balm to the burial place to complete Christ's entombment. When they arrived, they found the massive stone wheel at the entrance rolled away. The tomb was empty; Jesus was not there. Mary rushed off to tell Peter and John that their leader was gone. After doing so, she returned to the grave. The other women had remained at the tomb, and they fell to their feet at the appearance of an angel. Then they too ran off to find the disciples.

The first words of the resurrected King were uttered to Mary Magdalene after her return to the tomb. As she stood crying, the Messiah appeared and asked, "Woman, why do you weep? Who are you looking for?" (John 20:15 MSG). This simple woman of low status in society had the honor of being the first witness of the resurrected Lord. She was the first to hear His words and the first to be commissioned as He sent her to tell the disciples of His appearance.

The Ones Who Left

The hope of this Hebrew nation was that a Savior would come and rescue them from the evil clutches of Rome. The disciples and followers believed Jesus Christ was The One. Instead He dangled on a cross to His death, seeming to desert His beloved supporters.

After the betrayal and capture of their leader, most of the followers and disciples disappeared. Peter (and another unnamed disciple) did follow Jesus, only to deny Him three times and run away. John remained with the women.

These friends of Christ were left with fear for their safety, anxiety over their future, and engulfing grief. I imagine bitterness and anger also surged inside their inconsolable hearts.

After Christ's death, the disciples began to meet behind locked doors. On one of these occasions, the resurrected Messiah appeared. His first statement to His beloved was "Peace be with you." No disapproval or disappointment, no demand for explanations, only peace-filled words from the Prince of Peace.

These scared men who fled the scene of Jesus's death revolutionized the world after hearing Christ's powerful post-resurrection words of redemption. His courage filled them; His grace restored them. Heaven's heroes.

Will We Stay?

In the chronicles of the Christian church, stories of brave faith and martyrdom fill the pages—accounts of the those who stayed with Jesus. As His disciples in the Western world, we are not faced with a life-risking level of persecution. But the winds of change are blowing in as society shows less tolerance for biblical ideals and Christ-followers.

This Easter Sunday, may we count the cost as we look to the empty tomb. When the winds blow hot, may we find Him worth it all and be the ones who stay.

> Princes, kings, and other rulers of the world have used all their strength and cunning against the Church, yet it continues to endure and hold its own.[46]

---

46 John Foxe, *Foxe's Book of Martyrs* (Peabody, MA: Hendrickson Publisher, Inc., 2003).

Reflection

1. Which group do you identify the most with, the ones who stayed or the ones who left? Why?

2. How do the words of the resurrected Savior bring meaning and hope to your life today?

Prayer

Dear Savior,

Thank You for rising from the dead! I count the cost on this Easter Sunday as I look to the empty tomb. Jesus, may I be one who stays.

Amen

Days 41 and 42
The Risen Savior

The Day of Resurrection
(Verses 2 and 3)

Our hearts be pure from evil,
that we may see aright
the Lord in rays eternal
of resurrection light;
and listening to his accents,
may hear, so calm and plain,
his own "All hail!" and, hearing,
may raise the victor strain.

Now let the heavens be joyful!
Let earth the song begin!
Let the round world keep triumph,
and all that is therein!
Let all things seen and unseen
their notes in gladness blend,
for Christ the Lord hath risen,
our joy that hath no end.[47]

---

[47] St. John of Damascus; translator John Mason Neale, "The Day of Resurrection," 1800s.

#41

Do You Love Me?

When they had finished eating, Jesus said to Simon Peter,
"Simon son of John, do you love me more than these?"
John 21:15

Regret. Shame. A sense of failure. Perhaps you have made egregious mistakes, betrayed those you love, or failed at a job or relationship. Doubts creep in, and your faith feels shaky. Imagine Peter's state of mind after denying Christ three times in the courtyard (read Mark 14:66–72). Peter—the man who told his Master at the Last Supper that he would lay down his life for Him—wept bitterly.

After His resurrection, Jesus appeared many times to His disciples over the course of forty days. In John 21:1–14, we find seven disciples fishing in the Sea of Galilee, and the Savior shows up.

As I study this passage, I imagine myself in Peter's sandals, pushing a heavy wheelbarrow full of disgrace-laden bricks. What words would I need from Christ after betraying Him?

First, I would need a good lecture. Bring on the guilt trip! Second, I would crave an answer to the nonstop question swirling in my mind: *What use am I anymore?* Last, I would need Him to clear my name with those in the community who whispered about my betrayal. A public boost of my reputation after a most dramatic fall from grace.

Then I would humbly apologize and feel somewhat absolved.

But the Messiah didn't do any of these things. Over a breakfast fire with the one who denied Him three times, Jesus asked Peter, His friend of three years, one question.

"Do you love me?"

Three times He asked the same question.

In the Greek language, there are three words for "love." Two are used in the back-and-forth exchange between Jesus and Peter on the beach: *agape,* meaning "steady, deliberate, unconditional, intentional,"[48] and *philia,* meaning "affection, fondness shared by close friends or family."[49]

"Simon, do you *agape* Me more than these? (Is your love steady and unconditional)?"

"Yes, Lord, I *phileo* You (I am fond of You)."

"Tend My lambs."

"Simon, do you *agape* Me? (Is your love for Me deliberate and intentional?)".

"Yes, Lord. You know that I *phileo* You (I have great affection for You)."

"Shepherd My sheep."

"Simon, do you *phileo* Me? (Do you have great affection for Me)?"

"Lord, You know all things; You know that I *phileo* You (I have a great fondness for You)."

"Tend My sheep."

For Peter, the "these" Jesus referred to in the first question might have been the big haul of fish he had caught ... or something more profound. Perhaps the "these" could have been some things in Peter's life that were pulling him away from his calling in Christ.

---

48   James Strong, *The New Strong's Exhaustive Concordance of the Bible* (Nashville, TN: Thomas Nelson, 1995), 26.

49   James Strong, *The New Strong's Exhaustive Concordance of the Bible* (Nashville, TN: Thomas Nelson, 1995), 5373.

The questions around the fire were not a lecture or scolding. This back and forth on the beach was a recasting of a vision, to prepare Peter for a comeback. Christ caused Peter to reflect deeply on his love for his Master (a love that had been put to the flame) by asking these questions. Maybe the different uses of "love" were meant to shift Peter from *phileo* to *agape*. Jesus caused Peter to search his heart, to truly see where his allegiance lay.

Additionally, Jesus infused Peter's heart with grace, restoring and reinstating him. A preparation for the difficult ministry road ahead, which would be filled with persecution. Peter would soon have his own flock of believers to shepherd.

Imagine yourself by the fire with the Savior of Second Chances. Search your heart as He asks, "Do you love Me?" What do you say? Perhaps doubts and regret blur the grace you've been so freely given. Have disappointments dimmed the exuberance you used to have for Him? Are you pushing a weight of bricks filled with guilt? Where does your allegiance lie? With deeper intention comes obedience, not just lip service.

Take time in prayer and contemplation with your Savior. Today is the day to toss these feelings of shame into the fire. His grace is sufficient for our mistakes and doubts, and He is the God of not just second but countless chances.

Yes, Lord, I love You more than these.

Comebacks don't seem likely when your back is up against the wall and your hope is depleted. But if you will stay the course, you will discover God's power to reverse the irreversible in your life.[50]

---

[50] Tony Evans, "God gave me an incredible comeback—He can give one to you too," *Fox News*, April 14, 2018, https://www.foxnews.com/opinion/god-gave-me-an-incredible-comeback-he-can-give-one-to-you-too.

Reflection

1. In your journal, answer the questions in the last paragraph.

2. How might you practically express your love to God by caring for and leading others, shepherding and tending to His sheep?

Prayer

Dear Savior,

Like Peter, I have failed You. Countless times. Yet I stay the course of grace and believe You can reverse what seems irreversible in my life, and I will obey by caring for Your sheep. Thank You for Peter's story and Your constant mercy in my life. I love You more than anything!

Amen

#42

Famous Last Words

Jesus came up and spoke to them, saying, "All authority in
heaven and on earth has been given to Me. Go, therefore,
and make disciples of all the nations, baptizing them in
the name of the Father and the Son and the Holy Spirit,
teaching them to follow all that I commanded you; and
behold, I am with you always, to the end of the age."
Matthew 28:18–20 (NASB)

When someone is uttering their last words on earth, we pay
attention. These words are precious and important. This moment
is the final time we will hear their voice, see their face, or hold
their hand.

The passage for today, often called the Great Commission, is
a powerful one to end with on *our* last day together. This Scripture
is dear to me. As a college student, I put it to memory during a week
at a mountain camp. It was an intense time of seeking certainty in
God's purpose for my life. I got up in the predawn hours and hiked
to a boulder, where I sat and memorized these verses. Tears fell as
I considered how the Messiah's instructions to His disciples that
day two thousand years ago were for me too.

On His eleventh time to appear to His followers after the
resurrection, Christ and His eleven remaining disciples met on
a Galilean mountaintop. His final farewell. Here the resurrected

rabbi gave His men their closing instructions. What seemed like the end was really a beginning for these ordinary men on the cusp of even more extraordinary experiences. I imagine they stared intently at Him as they clung to His every word.

In the first part of this passage, we discover that God the Father gave Christ the Son all authority to commission His followers. Jesus repeatedly told His disciples of His authority and from whom it came. In Matthew 11:27 (HCSB), He explained, "All things have been entrusted to Me by My Father." These orders were not for global domination through violent means. They represented a glorious rescue plan.

Next we are told that the power of the Holy Spirit would be with His disciples. Acts 1:8 reads, "You will receive power when the Holy Spirit comes on you; and you will be my witnesses in Jerusalem, and in all Judea and Samaria, and to the ends of the earth." We receive power and strength to tell others about Christ from the Holy Spirit. We are to be His messengers in Jerusalem (our cities and neighborhoods), Judea and Samaria (our states and countries), and to the ends of the earth (anywhere God sends us).

Last but not least, the Messiah wants us to know we are not alone and that He will be with us *always*. Just moments before His ascension, He wanted to comfort His dear ones who had experienced loss, laughter, sorrow, fun, miracles, and every human emotion during their time with Him. Look what Christ promised in John 14:16–17: "I will ask the Father, and he will give you another advocate to help you and be with you forever—the Spirit of truth."

Dear friend, tears fall as I write this last chapter. I will miss you. Before we part, join me as we take to heart God's marching orders for us, these famous last words. Let us tell others about our Savior's story of grace and redemption and teach others about His Word, never forgetting that His power to do so lives in us. Forever.

When the Lord Jesus had finished talking with them,
he was taken up into heaven and sat down
in the place of honor at God's right hand.
Mark 16:19 (NLT)

Reflection

1. Look back on these forty-two days of studying the words
   of the Savior. Is there a particular passage or day that
   stirred you more than the rest? Commit to putting that
   verse (or verses) to memory.

2. Write a thank-you letter to Jesus for His words of saving
   grace, for His authority, and for His presence with you
   always.

Prayer

Dear Savior,

Thank You for our time together these last forty-two days, for
the intimate moments when You spoke to me in profound ways
and transformed me. May Your famous last words lead me to
passionately share Your message with those around me who don't
know You yet. I thank You for the power of the Holy Spirit living
in me and that You will be with me *always*.

Amen

Final Thoughts
and Thanks

Thank You, Jesus, for leading me here. My knowledge of and love for You has grown immensely through this book project. My life's purpose is to know You, make You known, and encourage others along the way.

Thank you, family and friends! Especially to you, Dan, for the editing, technical support, and patience with me. You cheered me on with each step, and it kept me going. To my kids: Samuel, Lauren, Noah, Josiah, and Micah, I am crazy about you. To Mom and Doug for always believing in me and my writing. To my sister, my Dolls, Kimberly (Ethel), Carrie, Sarah, James, and others, for your love and prayers during my darkest days. Where would I be without you? To Julian, "I Needed That."

To Sue Pic, Carrie V., Chris, and James for your kind endorsements.

To the Belletrists: there would be no book without you, and I am forever grateful. Who's next?

To the readers of my Purposeful Encouragement blog, thank you for reading my words and encouraging me with yours. Because you read, I write.

Finally, dear reader, thank you for taking this Easter journey with me, hearing our Savior. We did it!

For more connection, look for me here:

www.kristinsaatzer.com

@kmysaatzer

FACEBOOK.com/ENCOURAGEONPURPOSE

ORDER INFORMATION

REDEMPTION
P R E S S

To order additional copies of this book, please visit
www.redemption-press.com.
Also available at Christian bookstores, Amazon, and Barnes and Noble.